tuck

The Quilters' Guild Collection
Contemporary Quilts, Heritage Inspiration

The Quilters' Guild of the British Isles

EDITED BY BRIDGET LONG

David and Charles

A DAVID & CHARLES BOOK
Copyright © The Quilter's Guild of the British Isles 2005, 2008

David & Charles is an F+W Publications Inc. company
4700 East Galbraith Road
Cincinnati, OH 45236

First published in 2005
First UK paperback edition 2008

ISBN-13: 978-0-7153-1816-4 hardback
ISBN-10: 0-7153-1816-0 hardback

ISBN-13: 978-0-7153-2668-8 paperback
ISBN-10: 0-7153-2668-6 paperback

Printed in China by RR Donnelley
for David & Charles
Brunel House, Newton Abbot, Devon

Commissioning Editor: Vivienne Wells
Desk Editor: Ame Verso
Project Editor: Karen Hemingway
Executive Art Editor: Ali Myer
Senior Designer: Lisa Wyman
Production Controller: Ros Napper
Photography: Karl Adamson and Simon Whitmore

PICTURE CREDITS
All images joint copyright © David & Charles and The Quilter's Guild of the British Isles except:
p. 4, 6, 7, 8 top left, 10, 11, bottom, 14 top left, 15, 18, 23 bottom, 24 top and bottom, 26, 32 bottom, 48 bottom, 49, 52 top, 57 bottom left and middle right, 64 middle left, 65 top right, 70 bottom left, 72, 77, 79, 85 middle right, 93, 103 top right, 106, 109 top right courtesy of The Quilter's Guild of the British Isles, p. 55 bottom and 61 top centre and bottom right logo and newspaper report courtesy of the Chichester Observer, p. 56 bottom left Mike Watson, p. 92 bottom left Nigel Young, p. 100 middle left Laura Kemshall.

Visit our website at www.davidandcharles.co.uk

David & Charles books are available from all good bookshops; alternatively you can contact our Orderline on 0870 9908222 or write to us at FREEPOST EX2 110, D&C Direct, Newton Abbot, TQ12 4ZZ (no stamp required UK only); US customers call 800-289-0963 and Canadian customers call 800-840-5220.

CONTENTS

FOREWORD

The traditions of British quiltmaking go back centuries, through the thousands of anonymous quilters who have contributed to the varied techniques, styles and patterns. The aim of this book is to look back on this heritage (through quilts in The Quilters' Guild Collection) to enrich our quiltmaking future.

The Quilters' Guild is delighted to encourage quilters to develop their design skills, guided by the 12 outstanding teachers who have contributed to this book. We are grateful to these inspirational quilters for sharing their skills and knowledge, and to Bridget Long, for her excellent work throughout on planning, administering, co-ordinating and writing this book.

Finally, we should record the debt we owe members and staff who were instrumental in establishing and building the wonderful collection of quilts now owned by The Quilters' Guild. Without the hours they spent caring for those quilts, this book would not have been possible.

Fay Allwood
President, The Quilters' Guild of the British Isles, 2003–2005

INTRODUCTION

For today's quiltmakers, the work of the past can be seen as a vast resource for creating new work. The influential contemporary British quilter, Pauline Burbidge once said, 'I don't want to just throw off the traditions of quiltmaking, because I am close to that tradition and love being inspired by it. I am certainly inspired by the old quilts and like to show that inspiration through my work'.[1]

By recognizing the rich resource of British quilts and drawing on their distinctive characteristics, modern quilters can develop new and challenging designs for the future. Following that path, 12 contemporary quilters have taken inspiration from specific styles of quilt held in The Quilters' Guild museum collection to make their own very individual quilts for this book. To place them in their context, details of British quilt history accompany the quilts, with references to take the topics further.

Inspiration for Design

Many talented quilters may be frightened by the thought of design, assuming that leading quilters are somehow able to pluck designs out of the air. The 12 quilters featured in this book demonstrate that by following tried and trusted processes and routines, a quilt design can be developed from any object used for inspiration. The 12 projects show how varied the approaches can be, from drawing grids with pencil and paper or making paper collages, to using design software on

The House Blocks Quilt, 188 x 236cm (74 x 93in), The Quilters' Guild's first acquisition in 1979

a computer. The routines are explained and illustrated and, if experimented with, could give anyone the confidence to take a further step down the designing route. The featured designers' favourite techniques for dyeing or texturing cloth will help quiltmakers give their work even more individuality.

Many of the 12 quilters acknowledge that drawing is not their forte, so they follow design processes that do not need that skill. One even resorts to a computer to do the drawing work. All, however, are constantly keeping their eyes open for new things that intrigue and fascinate, spending time recording what they see. A lesson that any aspiring designer will take away from this book is the need to observe, collect and record. Collections of printed ephemera, found objects and photographs as well as drawings and sketches can be stored in an ideas book or file. Whilst some of the sketchbooks shown here are works of art in their own right, the basic principle to collect for inspiration can be applied to a simple file as well as a sketchbook.

Selection of sketchbooks from the contributing quilters

The Quilters' Guild and its Collections

The Quilters' Guild of the British Isles was formed in 1979 and is a national organization promoting quiltmaking across the United Kingdom. The Quilters' Guild aims to give quiltmaking the status it deserves both as a craft and as an art, and to encourage and maintain a high standard of workmanship and design. As a registered educational charity, The Quilters' Guild works to promote the appreciation, knowledge and understanding of the heritage, art and techniques of quiltmaking.

In the first few years of The Quilters' Guild's existence, a number of quilts and items of clothing were donated to form a small collection, which was used as study material for members. The first quilt was the House Blocks Quilt, consisting of blocks made by members of a previous organization, The Quilt Circle, including influential quilters and teachers such as Deirdre and Jean Amsden. The blocks were raffled and won by Jean, who made them into a quilt and donated it to the newly formed Quilters' Guild in 1979.

The growth of the collection was slow and unplanned, with only 18 items after five years. In 1990, The Quilters' Guild initiated a project documenting pre-1960s privately owned quilts and other items and the results of the British Quilt Heritage Project were published in 1995.[2] The book

marked a time when there was a growth in interest in British quilt history and, perhaps due to the raised profile of The Quilters' Guild, there was a rapid growth in the quilt collection, which has continued to the present day. The Quilters' Guild achieved full museum registration for its collection in 2001.

The collection now has over 450 large items, ranging from the oldest known dated patchwork to contemporary quilts commissioned from internationally and nationally known British quilt artists. The Quilters' Guild has a national collecting policy, collecting quilts and related items from across the British Isles to represent a broad range of styles, techniques and regional influences up to the present day. Striking quilts, clothing and domestic items from the 18th, 19th and 20th centuries are stored alongside tools, templates and fabrics. The need to collect the mundane as well as the wonderful is acknowledged, so recent acquisitions have included modern clothing in patchwork and quilting – and even a blue nylon quilted dressing gown.

Bridget Long

Up the Stairs, *100 x 100cm (39 x 39in)*, commissioned by Region 13 of The Quilters' Guild and made by Elizabeth Brimelow in 2004. Donated to the collection of contemporary quilts, celebrating 25 years of The Quilters' Guild

400 YEARS OF QUILTS

Four hundred years ago, people in Britain lived in a world of plain cloth. For the majority of them, the textiles available for clothing and furnishing were wool, linen, silk and the bast fibres such as hemp. All of these were available in plain colours because, although European textile manufacturers were skilled dyers and weavers, they lacked extensive skills to print pattern on cloth. Decorative weave silks were produced but, being expensive, were accessible only to the wealthier members of society. For centuries in Britain there had been a flowering of needlework and embroidery skills, which were used both in professional workshops and the domestic environment. People were able to use a variety of techniques such as fabric manipulation, punching, slashing, embroidery, quilting and inevitably probably patchwork to add pattern and texture to cloth in order to decorate their plain world.

Detail of the centre of the 1718 Silk Patchwork Coverlet

1718 Silk Patchwork Coverlet

The earliest known patchwork that bears a date is a silk patchwork coverlet dated 1718. Measuring 169 x 185cm (66½ x 73in), the 1718 Silk Patchwork Coverlet (opposite) consists of 182 figurative, geometric and decorative blocks of various sizes; the basic and smallest block size is 11 x 11cm (4½ x 4½in). In the central area of the upper half of the coverlet is a basic unit with the pieced date and initials 'E' and 'H' placed below a heart block and above figures of a man and woman with further heart motif blocks.

The whole coverlet has been pieced using paper templates. The fabric is wrapped over the templates and is tacked (basted) through the seam allowance and paper only, thus avoiding sewing through the top layer of silk. The pieces are joined together with fine hand oversewing (whip stitch) to create the blocks, which are then assembled in a complex grid design incorporating the various sizes of blocks. The paper templates have been left in place.

The entire coverlet is a tour de force of stitching. The individual blocks are often complex designs of figures, animals, birds and flowers made from a number of complicated shapes that require skilled hands to be sewn accurately and neatly. Many of the more difficult blocks are of the base unit size, which makes the individual components or pieces very small. To add to the complexity, the background behind many of the figurative blocks is diagonally quartered in contrasting fabrics, creating extra pieces for each block design.[1,2] The only embroidery used in the entire quilt is for the eyes of the animals.

The coverlet is laid out like a sampler and is patterned with motifs of domesticated animals and birds together with game such as deer, pheasants and partridges, reflecting the rural life of the family who owned it. It has passed through generations of farming gentry in Wiltshire but, sadly, extensive research has not revealed the owner(s) of the initials EH.[3] The fabrics, all of silk with the exception of a few pieces of wool/silk, wool/linen and silk/linen mix, appear to be almost all dress fabrics and many, dating from the 17th century, show signs of previous use.

1718 Silk Patchwork Coverlet, 169 x 185cm (66½ x 73in)

Detail from the 1718 Silk Patchwork Coverlet

this time. It is a misfortune that no earlier examples have survived. The survivors demonstrate the popularity of the half-square triangle shape in patchwork, used in diagonally quartered blocks or square on point designs. This simple shape continued to be seen extensively in silk patchwork right through the 18th century.

Texture on Plain Cloth

In the 18th century, quilting continued to be used for bedcovers and garments as before. Professional workshops supplied fashionable wadded and corded quilted items in silk and linen, whilst imported cotton quilting from Marseilles, France and India could be purchased from British shops. This trade was supplying the wealthier end of the market in which ornate textural quilted patterns were desirable for both furnishing and clothing.

The 18th-century fashion for dresses with an open front showing a petticoat, fed the trade in wadded silk petticoats to be bought off the peg or to order. The green silk petticoat shown below and containing the standard quilting patterns of flowers with wave motifs and zigzags seen on such 'mass-produced' garments, is typical of the styles available.[6]

The silk fabrics show that the owners had relatively high status, representing the merchant class, although the fabrics were not the best of the day. Only a few show flat metal strips, probably silver, woven as weft stripes in the silk; an indication of the costly cloth purchased and used by the wealthy classes.[4]

The 1718 Silk Patchwork Coverlet has been compared with a small number of other surviving silk patchwork items from the early 18th century, including a coverlet dated 1726 that is held in the collections of the McCord Museum of Canadian History, Montreal, Canada and came to Canada from Norwich, England.[5] All the items show a confidence in technique that would suggest that patchwork was widely known and used at

Utilitarian bedcovers and garments, incorporating basic quilting and patchwork, were likely to be made at the same time to provide both warmth and decoration. Sadly, evidence from this period does not exist for quilting activity in the lower social classes because the items would probably have been used to destruction rather than being stored away for future generations to find.

Silk quilted petticoat from the 18th century

The Blossoming of Patchwork

In 1609 William Finch, a far-sighted employee of the East India Company, suggested buying Indian-produced cloth such as muslins, pintadoes and quilts for sale in Britain. He was able to appreciate that the textile makers of India had achieved great skills in spinning and printing cottons, producing a cloth that would be a novelty in Europe.

Printed Indian cottons such as chintzes had an exotic look, provided by the large-scale flowing floral designs incorporating printed and painted motifs in strong red, blue, yellow, purple, black and orange, which the home textile manufacturers could not match. At first wealthier classes were reluctant to buy Indian cloth, although Samuel Pepys, the diarist bought a chintz dress for his wife in 1663 and had an informal robe for himself. However, by the end of the 17th century, wealthier ladies would wear chintz for upper garments as daywear, as well as undergarments, and chintz was used for bedcovers and wall hangings, thus establishing its fashionable status.

European linen and wool manufacturers saw the imported cottons as a threat and campaigned for a control and then a ban of imports, which many countries, including Britain, imposed in the late 1600s and early 1700s. Restrictions on the import of Indian cotton continued until 1774, although loopholes in the bans and illegal importation of cloth allowed Indian chintzes to be widely available throughout the century.

The famous Levens Hall, Cumbria patchwork quilt and bed curtain are made from imported Indian chintzes in an unembellished interlocking design of octagons, crosses, long hexagons and rectangles. Claimed by the family to be made in about 1708, the items are unlike the silk patchwork from the early 18th century, such as the 1718 Silk Patchwork Coverlet. Recent research has been unable to confirm the date, but the

Detail of plate print quilt from the late 18th century, owned by the Bell family of Kendal

Levens Hall pieces can still be regarded as the earliest patchwork made from printed cotton.[7]

European textile manufacturers faced with the threat of a desirable, novel product finally had to compete by developing printing skills on both linen and cotton and a home-based printing industry grew throughout the 18th century. As printed cotton and linen became available from European production, it was incorporated into patchwork. Rare survivors have been recorded from the mid-18th century such as the Clamshell patchwork bed hangings containing both Indian and European printed and painted cottons in the Victoria and Albert Museum, London.[8]

Towards the end of the century, cottons printed from wooden blocks (block prints) and from engraved copper plates (plate prints) were readily available but expensive and highly fashionable for both furnishing and dress. The detail of a late 18th-century wholecloth quilt, owned by the Bell family from Kendal (left), shows a plate print linen with a trellis of fine flowing flower stems with larger finely drawn flowers such as passionflowers, pinks and roses. It is quilted in double-lined Clamshell and Wineglass.

Cotton patchwork was a fashionable needlework technique and surviving examples are often intricate designs made by ladies who had access to many fabrics, possessed needlework and art design skills, and had time available to create complex patchwork, using the time-consuming technique of piecing over papers. Both the complex frame coverlet containing fabric from the 1795–1805 period (see pages 11 and 32) and the Mariner's Compass Coverlet (page 10) of a slightly later date are typical examples of the patchwork being produced. These items are very often unquilted coverlets rather than quilts, suggesting they were more for show than for functional bedcovers. The Mariner's

Mariner's Compass Coverlet, 252 x 273cm (99 x 108in), a pieced coverlet
with a compass pattern centre from the early 19th century

Compass Coverlet (opposite) has a very complex compass pattern pieced centre and is surrounded by diamonds of printed cottons and linens alternating with plain and dimity (containing a textural weave) cotton.

Panels block printed on to fabric lengths were cut and sold for use in patchwork or for cushions (pillows) and fire screens. They were often produced to commemorate important events such as George III's Golden Jubilee in 1810, Wellington's victory at Waterloo in 1815, or the wedding of Princess Charlotte of Wales and Leopold Prince of Saxe Coburg in 1816. Others were pleasing designs incorporating flowers, birds, baskets and figures such as the unused panel of feeding birds in a nest shown on the right and the eight panels in the quilt on page 13.

right Block-printed panel c. 1820

Detail of complex frame coverlet of 1795–1805

The Influence of Technology

In the early 19th century, technological developments were influencing the production techniques for printing cotton. Until then, printed cotton was aimed at the quality end of the market on the basis of cost. Block printing is a very time-consuming process involving a separate carved wooden block for each colour used in the design. Producing detailed, high-quality single colour with white designs, plate printing from engraved copper plates was also expensive because of the high cost of creating the plates.

In 1783, Thomas Bell of Glasgow developed a technique of engraved cylinder printing (printing using a metal roller), allowing the production of continuous lengths of printed cloth. Although not used until the 19th century, the roller-printing process allowed the development of new print styles that could not be achieved by the other two print processes and this, coupled with lower production costs, saw the popularity of printed cotton grow. Through the first decades of the century, the patterns became more and more complex as printers developed their skills of manipulating printing methods and dyeing techniques.

The growth of cotton production is reflected in the quilts and coverlets seen in the first half of the 19th century. No longer just the province of leisured ladies, cotton patchwork quilts were widely made as cotton became cheaper and more abundant. The quilts at this time were often simpler in design, most being made in an all-over mosaic or a frame style,

Detail of the centre of the frame quilt dated 1844; the appliqué probably dates from the 1820s

reflecting the possible lack of artistic or drafting skills or even the time available to devote to the needlework. Patchwork was no longer mainly pieced over paper template shapes; the technique of seaming patchwork pieces with a running stitch was also used. Typical of the quilts made, the colourful frame quilt shown opposite is signed in the centre, 'JH Thorne September 3 1824', and is a mix of roller and block-printed dress cottons pieced in simple squares and rectangles. At its centre and on one of the outer frames are block-printed panels with a gothic ruin and flowers. It is heavily quilted in a frame design unrelated to the frame patchwork pattern.[9]

Patchwork was often quilted at this time, but the quilting layout tends to be unrelated to the pieced design. All-over quilting patterns such as Clamshell or straight lines in a zigzag were used, but the centre and frame-quilting layout with defined borders was common throughout the first half of the 19th century as seen in the Cockburn wholecloth quilt (see page 78).

Unlike Broderie Perse appliqué, which relied on printed motifs to provide the design, appliqué became more creative with individual designs often in a naïve style as seen in the centre of the frame quilt shown above. Dated 1844, the delightful appliqué centre, showing birds sitting on a rudimentary tree in a pot, was likely to have been made in the mid-1820s. It was probably finished with fabrics printed later, when the outer block design was added in the 1840s.

Frame quilt, 246 x 292cm (97 x 115in), inscribed 'JH Thorne September 3 1824'

above Detail of Painted Silks Hexagon Coverlet,
112 x 163cm (44 x 64in), from the late 19th century

above Detail of pieced strippy quilt, *243 x 234cm
(95½ x 92in),* from 1880–1900 in cotton and wool

Fashion and Utility

The different styles of quilt made in the second half of the 19th century are exemplified by the two pieces illustrated in detail here. Measuring 112 x 163cm (44 x 64in), the small coverlet or cover (left) is made from a variety of colourful, patterned silk hexagon rosettes set very effectively against a black silk hexagon background. The white centre to each rosette shows a small hand-painted flower. It has a border of silk diamonds with applied cords and braids and a deep multicoloured fringed border.

The dark-coloured quilt (below, left) with deep purple plain strips dividing pieced squares on point, contains a mix of wools and cottons. Made around 1880–1900 in the north east of England, it is a large bed quilt measuring 243 x 234cm (95½ x 92in) and is strip quilted with Cable border patterns and rose motifs on the squares. The quilt is very striking but simply made with many joined fabrics in the squares and an uneven shape to the finished piece.

The two pieces come from different worlds. The small silk coverlet was sewn by someone with access to luxury fabrics, who could afford to use cords, braids and fringes for ornament. The hexagons and diamonds are hand pieced over paper templates and the painted flowers are painstakingly worked. The cover is a showy piece made by a needlewoman with time to spend on patchwork, living in a stylishly furnished house where the cover would be on display. The pieced strippy quilt provided warmth for a bed and was made from the fabrics that were readily available to the quiltmaker. It is part of a tradition of patchwork and quilting in an area where finances are likely to have restricted the time spent quilting and the choice of fabrics used.

This split in quilt styles was led in part by a further revolution in textile production. In 1856, WH Perkin discovered the first synthetic dye from coal tar – a bright purple called 'mauveine'. Perkin's mauve was followed very quickly by other new aniline dyes, which were far more suitable for use on protein fibres such as silks and wools, rather than cotton. Throughout the century, printed cottons had moved down the social scale as they became cheaper. As the status of cotton declined, so silk again became more important. The novelty of the new bright coloured dyes on silks led to their predominance in fashion, especially in the last quarter of the 19th century. The silks were used for many

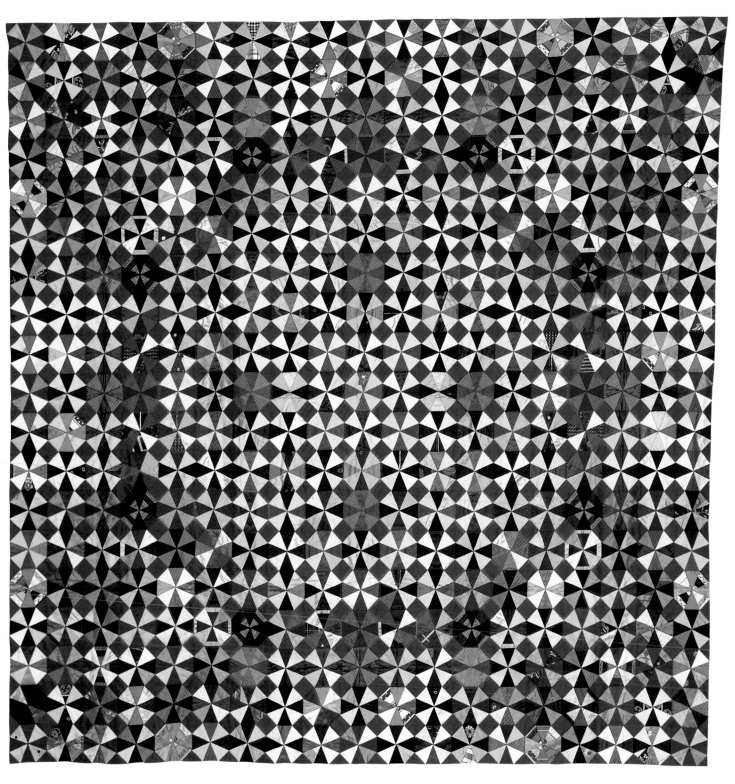

Kaleidoscope pattern mosaic quilt, *216 x 220cm (85 x 86½in)*,
made in silk by Elizabeth Watson of Cumbria in the late 19th century

Medallion Crazy Coverlet, *200 x 213cm (79 x 84in),* made in silk and velvet by Frances Maria Fletcher (née Cope) for her wedding in 1873

was some resentment amongst the sisters who remained on the farm, especially as they had a new dress only once a year, made from a practical fabric of sombre colour.

Cotton quilts made at this time often testify to the thrift of the maker. Quilts were often simple in design, relying on quilting on large areas of plain fabric to provide the textural interest. Fabrics were frequently the widely available household cottons such as Turkey Red and white cottons seen in the Red and White Quilt (see page 38); many were recycled and, if purchased, were often obtained cheaply as fents or discarded sample books.

The simple cotton frame quilt seen opposite has four pieced borders of rectangles, the shape typical of sample books, showing many similar cotton print designs including some with different colourways. The centre of this quilt is an octagon containing larger pieces of furnishing cotton, some patterned with Art Nouveau inspired motifs. Cottons seen in quilts at this time have been mass-produced with repetitive often unoriginal designs. Influences such as the Art and Crafts Movement or Art Nouveau are not often seen in the patterns on cotton fabric for this type of market.

Simple cotton fabrics were often used for group projects, producing quilts as gifts or for fundraising. Bazaar quilts, usually two-coloured red and white or blue and white, raised money for church or chapel funds through the sale of patches in a quilt. The pieces were signed by the purchaser and embroidered before being incorporated into the quilt.

patchwork pieces during this time, as can be seen with the Irish Crazy Patchwork Coverlet (see page 71) and the Jubilee Quilt (see page 72), the Silk Triangles Coverlet (see page 90) and the Silk Log Cabin Table Cover (see page 46).

Three Watson sisters lived on a large farm in Cumbria at the end of the 19th century. After getting up at 5.00am to do their chores, they spent time sewing during daylight hours, particularly after lunch. They were prolific quilters, making both utilitarian quilts for the farm workers and finer pieces such as the dazzling silk Kaleidoscope pattern mosaic quilt shown on page 15, made by Elizabeth Watson for her 'bottom drawer' (although she never married).

Francis Maria Fletcher (née Cope) made the diamond, star and crazy coverlet shown above before her wedding in 1873, when she lived on a farm in Belper, Derbyshire. It is likely that she sourced the silk and velvets for the coverlet from her sister who was a buyer for a London fashion house and probably had access to fashionable fabrics. The family story is that there

Detail of signature quilt from Jarrow on Tyne made in 1897, made to celebrate Queen Victoria's Diamond Jubilee

Frame quilt, 222 x 235cm (87 x 93in), from the late 19th century, in cotton including samples

The white, blue and red cotton quilt bearing an embroidered portrait of Queen Victoria (left) in her Diamond Jubilee year in 1897, was made in Tyneside. Measuring 222cm (87in) square, it is inscribed 'Primitive Methodist Connexion Jarrow on Tyne Circuit' above and '1837 Diamond Jubilee 1897' below the portrait. The quilt features over 210 embroidered names including TT Harvey Circuit Steward and the Reverends C Seaman, J Atkinson and C Phillipson. It is unknown whether the quilt was made just in commemoration of the Jubilee or also to raise funds for the Methodist Church.

A Distinctive Style

The striking quilt shown opposite is simply made from plain wool. The harmonious use of strong deep colours, a simple patchwork frame design with a star in the centre and deeply incised quilting set off by the multicoloured prairie point edge are combined in a very pleasing effect.

Thought to have been made by Mrs Megan Jones at the end of the 19th or beginning of the 20th century, this quilt has a simple patchwork design enhanced by a centre and defined frame quilting layout that is typical of Welsh quilts of the period. In the first half of the 19th century, the centre and defined frame layout was ubiquitous, being used across the whole country. Welsh quilts continued to be quilted in this style, but in the north of England, quilt designers influenced the development of a much looser undefined frame style in the second half of the 19th century (see page 77).

The layout here consists of a large circle enclosed in a central square. The surrounding borders are separated by lines (defined) and contain quilt motifs such as leaves, spirals, four-petal flowers and pairs of Welsh Scissors. Welsh quilting motifs have a distinct character which, when combined with a defined framed layout, provide clues as to the likely provenance of the quilt.

The classic Welsh quilting layout can be seen in the bright blue wool and yellow cotton strippy (left). This also contains traditional quilting motifs such as a Wheel, Fans, Church Windows and spirals. Unlike strippies from the north of England (see page 101), Welsh strippies do not commonly have a strippy quilting pattern. The defined framed style is also seen in the two later quilts made for Claridges Hotel (see pages 22 and 23). Welsh quilts of the 20th century, made under the Rural Industries Bureau scheme, tend to have very precisely drafted patterns and accurately drawn framed layouts, indicating the high standards expected under the scheme, but they perhaps do not have the attraction of the more individual quilts made before that time.

Welsh strippy quilt, *195 x 213cm (77 x 84in),* from the early 20th century

Welsh wool frame quilt, *198 x 204cm (78 x 80in),*
from the 19th or the beginning of the 20th century

Decline and Revival in the 20th Century

During the first two decades of the 20th century, the impact of World War I and changes in fashion affecting domestic textiles led to a decline in quiltmaking. Commercially produced woven cotton covers, machine-made 'Marcella' quilts, wool coverlets and eiderdowns were popular alternatives for beds. However, there was still a need for warm bedcovers, as demonstrated by the unusual and striking yellow and white quilt shown opposite, which is unwashed so it still has the blue pencil markings probably made by a quilt designer. It is likely to have been made in around 1910 in the Castleside area of County Durham, northern England. The quilting motifs along the large central diagonal cross shapes and the borders are well-known strippy/border designs, including Weardale Chain, Cable Twist and Plait, together with roses, freehand feathers and scrolling.

The rectangular red and white Star quilt shown right is from the same period, but its provenance is unknown. It varies from the standard square Star design attributed to Elizabeth Sanderson, with the central pieced star floating in a wide central rectangle and a reduced number of borders.

At this time, quilts were often made by itinerant quilters who worked for a daily rate, including food and lodging.[10] More were supplied by village quilters or from quilt clubs. Quiltmaking tended to be concentrated in only a few areas of Britain, particularly South Wales and the north east of England. In the industrial and mining areas in both these regions, quilt clubs operated as a regular source of income for families in straitened circumstances.[11, 12] The clubs had regular customers who paid for their quilts by subscription over a number of weeks. Quilts were delivered to the club members in turn and lots were often drawn for the order in which they were to be delivered. The quilter made a profit of about £1 to £1.10s (£1.50) on each quilt.[13]

In the late 1920s and 1930s, there was a determined effort by a number of organizations to revive quilting as a way of providing income for families. The Rural Industries Bureau worked with Mavis FitzRandolph to regenerate the quilting tradition in both South Wales and the north of England, drawing on the skills of existing quilters and establishing classes for new workers. Quilts, cushions (pillows), dressing gowns and bed jackets were made to order and were often sold through London shops such as the Little Gallery run by Muriel Rose.[14] A famous order was placed by Claridges Hotel, London for quilts and pillowslips for rooms in their new Art Deco style extension. Fifty quilters from South Wales and County Durham were involved in completing the order, some groups making a pair of large quilts with pillow covers to match in only one week.[15] The two well-used quilts seen on pages 22 and 23 (both made in South Wales) are survivors of this large order; they were rediscovered by the hotel in 1980 and donated to The Quilters' Guild. The peach coloured quilt reversing to blue is quilted in a classic Welsh centre and defined borders layout, with typical Welsh motifs. The cream quilt seen in detail is also quilted in a centre and defined borders layout, but with a signature lotus motif taken directly from the Art Deco style of the building.

Star pattern quilt, 209 x 225cm (82 x 89in), in Turkey Red and white cotton from the early 20th century

Triple X Quilt, *226 x 241cm (89 x 95in), in yellow and white cotton sateen, c. 1910*

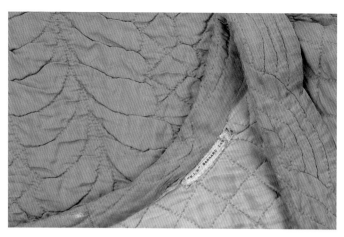

Detail of the blue silk dressing gown made in the Northern Industries Workroom, Barnard Castle in the early 1930s, showing the embroidered nametape

Whilst the Rural Industries Bureau scheme generated orders for quilts to be made in quilters' homes or at classes, the Northern Industries Workrooms established two places of work in Barnard Castle and Langley Moor near Durham in the early 1930s, where employees could complete orders for quilts and other items. Girls and young women learned to quilt at the workrooms and then made quilts, dressing gowns, cushions (pillows) and tea cosies in silks and satin. A blue silk dressing gown with a soft wool filling, now very fragile because of constant use since it was made, still bears the embroidered nametape showing its origin in one of the workrooms.[16]

The Quakers were also involved with helping to relieve the hardship of people living in the mining valleys of South Wales. Through the initiative of Emma Noble, a Quaker from Swindon, Wiltshire, a centre was opened in the Rhondda Valley, South Wales, offering cultural, leisure and adult educational programmes. Sewing and quilting were important parts of the lives of women who attended the centre and, although most of the quilts were made for personal use, some were sent to London for sale.[17]

Between World War I and II, quilting was still used as a means of fundraising. Church Guilds in Hawick in the Scottish Borders worked all year round on quilts, which were then sold for church funds in an annual two-day sale in the town hall. Although close to the quilting communities of Northumberland and Durham, with their distinctive layout style and preferred motifs, the quilters developed their own designs, creating a distinctive 'Hawick' look. The blue cotton sateen quilt (shown opposite), one of 30 quilts made by Janet Pow in the late 1920s and 1930s, contains four hearts in the centre with a border of hearts on the quilt edge. The remainder of the quilt is infilled with Clamshell and not the more typical Square Diamond infill. The hearts are typically Hawick style, with spiky leaf centres. Other motifs favoured by Hawick quilters include thistles and scalloped borders.

Detail of machine-made Comfy quilt showing the commercial label

Detail of Welsh wholecloth quilt made for Claridges Hotel, showing a lotus flower motif on the borders

A great threat to the handmade quilt was the machine-made Comfy quilt. Instantly recognizable by its small size, regular zigzag machine quilting and bordered layout, often with a diamond centre, the Comfy was produced extensively, judging by the numbers that survive. It was made to be reversible with both sides containing a centre and borders of alternating plain and patterned cottons. Sadly, no records of the company making the Comfy have ever been found, but it was one of a number of factory-made quilted bedcovers that contributed to the decline of the individually designed and worked quilt.

left Wholecloth quilt, *193 x 213cm (76 x 84in),* made in cotton sateen by Mrs Janet Pow of Hawick, Scottish Borders, in the late 1920s or early 1930s, with detail of central heart motifs *above*

Welsh cotton wholecloth quilt, *196 x 226cm (77 x 89in),* made for Claridges Hotel under the Rural Industries Bureau scheme in the early 1930s

In the Hour of Need

Any study of British quilt history is not complete without a group of quilts that were not even made in Britain. During World War II, volunteers in a number of allied countries made efforts to help the British cause, and many contributions of aid such as clothing, bandages and bedding were shipped to Britain. The Canadian Red Cross was a leading contributor to the war effort, supplying many items made strictly to standardized patterns and samples in sewing rooms across the country. Quilts were an exception to the standardization, as noted in a report by the Canadian National Women's Work Committee chairman, Mrs C McEachren: 'One outstanding exception where no samples were required should be noted, namely the patchwork quilts which were made by hundreds of Canadian women in their own homes. They went overseas by the thousand and proved a boon to the British people, especially when the air raids began.'[18] Edmonton Red Cross workers and country branches made 3,231 quilts in 1942 and Nova Scotia alone sent 24,149 quilts between 1941 and 1945.[19]

The quilts and other supplies were shipped into Britain and distributed through the British Red Cross Society, the Women's Voluntary Service (now the Women's Royal Voluntary Service) and the Salvation Army. The quilts were given to people made homeless through enemy bombing or strategic relocation, and to refugees, hospitals and the armed forces. Surviving recipients of the quilts remember overwhelming feelings of warmth towards the generous quilters from the other side of the Atlantic. Many made homeless by bombing, having lost all possessions, recall being given quilts as a first contribution towards a new life.

The surviving quilts can be recognized by a woven or printed label in red and white reading 'Gift of the Canadian Red Cross Society', which was machine stitched to one corner of the quilt back. Because they were not made to pattern, they

Detail of Canadian Red Cross quilt showing special V for Victory fabric

could contain a variety of block patchwork patterns showing the taste of the maker. They were made from dress cottons, wools and the new artificial silks of the period. However, many of the quilts were made from simple unembellished Crazy patchwork set in blocks with sashing, as seen in the quilt above, which features two special fabrics with a red or a blue background printed with large white Vs (for Victory) and the Morse code for V: dot-dot-dot-dash. However, many of these quilts were made from more utilitarian fabrics such as striped pyjama fabric or cotton feed/flour sacks.

The quilt made from five vertical bands of randomly pieced strips of a mixture of fabrics, shown right, unusually indicates where the quilters were based. Embroidered in the middle of the central strip is 'Hallville Ont(ario) R(ed) Cross'.

Detail of the Canadian Red Cross Society label

above Canadian Red Cross quilt, *185 x 152cm (73 x 60in),* from Hallville, Ontario

Another Canadian organization called the Imperial Order of the Daughters of the Empire also contributed to the war effort. Founded in 1900 by Mrs Clark Murray to encourage patriotism and social service, the order was open to all Canadian women with a British connection. Chapters of the order united in a common cause and sent clothing parcels mostly comprising of knitted garments and socks to Britain during both world wars. A quilt has been recorded bearing the label 'I.O.D.E.', but it is unknown how extensively members made quilts.

Wholecloth quilt, *220 x 262cm (87 x 103in)*, made by Amy Emms
in 1993 from acetate satin with polyester wadding

Keeping the Flame Alive

After World War II, patchwork and quilting fell out of favour. They were associated with recycling, thrift and making-do, all deeply unfashionable concepts in an era when people were trying to forget rationing and hardship. Women preferred candlewick bedcovers and eiderdowns. A few determined women quilters continued, especially in South Wales and the north east of England, and the skills were passed on at quilt groups formed by the Rural Industries Bureau and at classes.

Amy Emms was one of these exceptional women. Born in 1904 in County Durham, Amy grew up steeped in the tradition of quilting, working alongside her mother to make quilts for a quilt club and for shops in the local town. She continued to quilt after the war, teaching quilting to others so that it 'never became a dying craft' and was awarded an MBE (Member of the Order of the British Empire) for her outstanding contribution to the craft of quilting. She personally took on responsibility for maintaining the traditions of north-country quilting and was often seen at exhibitions and quilt shows demonstrating her skills up to her death in 1998. Her 1993 quilt (left), commissioned by The Quilters' Guild, is a typical example of the fine design and stitch work for which she was known.

Jessie Edwards, another quilting legend, was the teacher of the Porth, Rhondda group, set up by the Rural Industries Bureau in South Wales before World War II. She took part in a quilt exhibition held at the Welsh Folk Museum in 1951,

Detail of cotton quilt with wool wadding made by Jessie Edwards in 1959

in an attempt to revive interest in quilting, and continued to teach and make quilts to order. A detail of one of her quilts made in 1959 (above) shows the complex nature of her quilt designs and the closely worked quilting stitches.

The influential British quilt historian and quiltmaker, Averil Colby published three books on patchwork and quilting in the mid-20th century at a time when the crafts were disregarded. She had a clear influence over British patchwork of the period, developing a style incorporating many floral fabrics in hexagons and diamonds, which were pieced over papers to make complex flower bouquets, swags and wreaths. Her style was copied particularly through the National Women's Institute where she was chairman of the Handicrafts committee from 1956–61, resulting in a very 'English' look to patchwork at this time.[20] After her death in 1983, her remarkable fabric collection, dating from the end of the 18th to the 20th century, was given to The Quilters' Guild. It now forms the basis of the Averil Colby Fabric Collection.

Pincushions and samples made by Averil Colby with fabric from her collection

THE PROJECTS

Frame Coverlet, 249 x 283cm (98 x 111in), believed to have been made by Esther Cooper Cockram Perry in the 1830s

The floral frame coverlet (opposite) is believed to have been made in the 1830s by Esther Cooper Cockram Perry, but it could possibly have been made by her aunt, who was also called Esther Cooper. Esther was married to Reverend Perry of Seighford, near Stafford. A large piece, this coverlet is made from four distinctive highly glazed furnishing cottons, three of which are large-scale, flowing, flower designs, each with a different coloured background of white, blue or dark brown black. The fourth fabric is a large-scale floral stripe on a blue background. Eight large half-square triangles make up the central square, which is surrounded by three pieced borders made from squares on point and triangles, and two borders of fabric with no piecing.

FRAME QUILT
ANNETTE MORGAN

Annette Morgan has created this striking modern frame quilt Framed Taos (right) in response to the Esther Cooper coverlet (opposite). Using techniques such as collage and brainstorming to develop ideas, she has translated the coverlet's key motifs of zigzags, triangles and squares using modern methods of machine appliqué, machine quilting, fabric painting and microwave dyeing.

'I'm no good at drawing – give me a piece of paper and some scissors and I am fine.'

ANNETTE MORGAN

Annette was originally drawn to quiltmaking, not for the design potential of the craft, but 'because it covered a variety of techniques that a competent needlewoman could specialize in'. Though she trained as a nurse, Annette has made her career in quiltmaking, becoming one of Britain's leading teachers and award-winning quilt makers. Ideas are more abundant than time, so Annette uses the quick methods of machine quilting and appliqué, together with foundation piecing. (Foundation piecing is a quick but highly accurate method of sewing fabric pieces together, generally by machine, by following sewing lines marked on a foundation base of cloth or paper.) She also enjoys hand quilting when she has more time.

Internationally known quilters such as Ruth B McDowell, Caryl Bryer-Fallert, Jo Budd and Jane Sassaman provide inspiration, but Annette has established her own distinct style, drawing on her interest in social issues such as the Indian suttee tradition and seeking stimulation from landscapes or ethnic and tribal artefacts.

Frame Quilts

The frame style has been popular in British quilting for three centuries. British quilters created frame quilts using a special fabric, printed panel or strong pieced or appliqué motif for the centre, surrounded by pieced and plain borders. The British Quilt Heritage Project, documenting privately owned quilts (run by The Quilters' Guild 1991–93),

Complex frame coverlet, *215 x 215cm (84 x 84in)*, probably made in Yorkshire c.1795–1805

revealed that about 15 per cent of the recorded pieced quilts were of the frame style, showing its popularity over time.[1]

Frame quilts can be as simple or as complicated as quilters choose to make them, but if the frames are pieced, a good grasp of arithmetic and drafting skills are needed to fit the patchwork motifs accurately within the frames' dimensions. Many of the surviving frame quilts have striking designs, but the patchwork motifs in the frames are incomplete, suggesting that the maker, although a skilled needlewoman, was not able to calculate the required size of the repeated patchwork shape. Perhaps one of the attractions of the frame style was that quilters could sew patchwork strips independently and only later bring the frames together to make the whole quilt.

Complex frame quilts had many borders, each with elaborate pieced patterns. This is typified by a coverlet from c.1795–1805 (left), believed to have been made in Yorkshire, that features 15 frames fitted into its comparatively small size of 215cm (84in) square. Such a coverlet, entirely hand pieced over paper templates, can only have been made by someone with good sewing and drafting skills, and large amounts of leisure time. Later in the 19th century, much simpler utilitarian frame quilts were pieced by machine or hand running stitch, as the makers came from a level of society where time was not so freely available for quiltmaking.

INSPIRATION, RESEARCH AND BRAINSTORMING

Annette is finding new connections between her work and the traditional frame design. She says, 'I like working with the freedom of appliqué and so when I was approached to make a frame quilt [for this project] I was a little surprised. I had made a few pieces that had borders and frames, but I had not considered that these related to the old style of frame quilts. However, the more I pursued the idea of frame quilts, the more I saw that it related to my own work.'

After a trip to Santa Fe, USA, Annette made a series of quilts called Taos Trail. They all featured a zigzag motif drawn from scrapbook and brainstorming exercises, inspired by the frequent lightning storms over the Sangre de Cristo mountains, as well as motifs she saw in Native American jewellery and costume.

When studying British frame quilts, she had also noticed a zigzag pattern often occurring in the frame borders, as we can see in the Esther Cooper coverlet. So she decided to follow the ideas through from the Taos Trail series to create a new design inspired by the frame style.

Annette designs intuitively; after preparatory research, the ideas are allowed to grow through the design process. When a quilt design is drawn from specific source material, Annette collects as many images as possible to give a feel for the subject. These include her own photographs and sketches, together with materials in books, magazines, guides and brochures. Once immersed in a scrapbook of images, she feels ready to brainstorm the colours, shapes, textures and patterns that have become the defining features of the topic. The brainstorming process can help a designer confirm impressions gained during the 'immersion' stage. At its simplest, brainstorming can be time put aside to write down words that freely come to mind when considering the subject. For Annette, the results of a brainstorming session may be a large piece of paper with the topic word at the centre surrounded by defining words, colour patches and sketches of shapes, which are in turn circled by other words taking the description of the topic further (right).

Taos Trail 11 by Annette Morgan, 96 x 96cm (48 x 38in), created in response to her experiences in Santa Fe

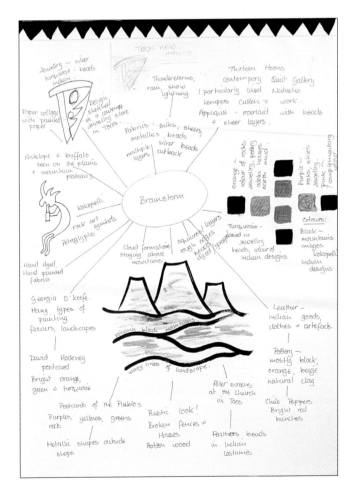

Annette's brainstorm sheet from the Santa Fe trip

Coloured textured papers from which
Annette begins her creative process

Collage impression of the Esther Cooper
coverlet, using coloured textured papers

Collage from the Esther Cooper coverlet
study, also drawing on the Santa Fe study

For this project, Annette looked at as many pictures as she could find of old frame quilts and came up with a list of their features. These included: lots of borders, squares, half-square triangles, medallion centre, zigzag patterns and flowery fabric. She then compared this list with specific features in the Esther Cooper coverlet: the centre square, the triangles set to form a zigzag border, the stripes on the outer border and the colours black, blue, red and green.

DESIGNING WITH TEXTURED PAPER COLLAGE

After the brainstorming, Annette made a textured paper collage (middle left) to give a loose impression of the Esther Cooper coverlet. Such 'paper and scissors collages' are useful to reproduce the impressions created by the brainstorming and then to develop designs from those impressions. Coloured, textured papers can be made easily by marking patterns on coloured paper using brushes, rollers, sponges or blocks, with a variety of paints.

The collages are made by cutting or even tearing the papers to produce shapes, which can be built up to reflect the topic. These could be a free interpretation of a specific image or key shapes arising from the brainstorming.

At this stage Annette was able to pinpoint certain shapes or colour combinations in the collages that she liked enough to develop further – experimenting with changes of scale, spacing, orientation and placement.

Then, drawing on the design work inspired by her Santa Fe trip and the Taos Trail series as well as the Esther Cooper coverlet, she tried more collages before she found a design that she felt had movement, colour and excitement.

She tried other colour schemes such as red, orange, yellow and black which were more related to the Santa Fe ideas (bottom left), but the final design is based on the black, blue, red and green colours of the Esther Cooper coverlet.

During this process of immersion, brainstorming and collage-making, intuition is key for designers like Annette, who is looking for pleasing design elements that she wants to take further. The benefit of such a process is that there is always plenty of unused material to return to when looking for more ideas.

COLLAGE TO CLOTH

Framed Taos went straight from collage to cloth with only some tinkering around to improve the spacing between the motifs and to scale up the collage to a wall hanging. The final collage seemed cramped, so Annette moved the shapes further apart. The collage's colour scheme was retained and Annette decided to reproduce the look of some of the textured papers by painting cotton fabric with acrylic paints. These she applied both by roller and by sponging paint on to the cotton through a thin piece of metal mesh. Acrylic paints do tend to stiffen the fabric, but she considered that this was acceptable in a piece of work intended as a wall hanging.

Annette likes the effect she can achieve by hand dyeing and painting her own fabrics – in this project only the black fabric was commercially produced. She prefers the uneven finish of hand-dyed fabrics to the defined printed images and regular repeat patterns of commercial fabrics. The yellow background fabric was dyed using Dylon cold-water dye before being roller painted with green acrylic. The turquoise-blue and red fabrics were microwave-dyed using Omega Dyrect dyes for cellulose fibres. The turquoise was then sponged with a darker blue acrylic paint.

above Textured papers
below Matching painted fabrics

MICROWAVE DYEING

The bucket dyeing methods often used by quilters for dyeing (for example, with fibre reactive cold-water dyes) need substantial amounts of space and can be messy. Annette is a great fan of microwave dyeing because she can dye quite small amounts of fabric very quickly in each microwave session, as follows.

YOU WILL NEED

Large strong plastic bag
(freezer bags are ideal)

5ml (1tsp) salt

3–5ml (½–1tsp) Omega Dyrect
dye powder (amount depends on
strength of colour required)

30ml (1fl oz) cold water
to dissolve dye

0.25m (¼yd) fabric to be dyed
(pre-soaked in water until all
the fibres in the fabric appear
to have taken up the water and
then squeezed gently to get rid
of excess water)

Fixing agent such as Synthrapol
or similar

METHOD

1. Put the salt, dye and cold water into the plastic bag.
2. Add the pre-soaked cotton fabric.
3. Squeeze the bag to distribute the dye powders into the fabric fibres. If required, add a little more water to help distribute the dye through the fabric.
4. Place the unsealed bag, opening upwards, in a dish or a strong ice cream container.
5. Microwave on high power for approximately five minutes.
6. Wash and rinse the fabric in soapy water until the water is clear of colour. If the colour bleeds, use a commercial fixing agent such as Synthrapol in the final rinse.

Rectangular reworking of the final quilt design in collage, showing how the ideas can be taken further

CONSTRUCTION

The final design of Framed Taos still features some of the pieced motifs of the Esther Cooper coverlet, such as the zigzag triangles and the squares, but these float freely on a black background. This made it possible to use the easy machine appliqué technique to construct the quilt. The motifs, taken from the final collage, were bonded to the black background fabric using a fusible web (such as Bondaweb), which is ironed to the back of the motifs and to the quilt top. The edges of the motifs were machined using blanket stitch to neaten the raw edges. The whole piece was machine quilted very simply with outline quilting around the motifs and an infill of unevenly spaced straight lines on the black background. Annette chose to make the edges of the quilt uneven since she felt that this was more in keeping with her design. Her final comment: 'I have to say that I became quite excited by the new work and can't wait until I have more time to move the designs on further.'

Chintz

Detail of the Esther Cooper coverlet showing chintz fabric

During the 18th and early part of the 19th century, the term 'chintz' described both dress and furnishing fabrics printed with the full range of colours that could be achieved at that time, using a variety of mordants with red, yellow and blue dyes. The word 'chintz' is actually derived from the Indian word 'chint', for spotted cloth, and relates back to the cottons that were imported from India throughout the previous two centuries.

At this time, both dress and furnishing fabrics were glazed by the calendering process (passing the cloth between heavy rollers, which smoothes and glazes the cloth by applying pressure to the fabric); a very practical process designed to repel dirt. Calendering was abandoned for dress fabric by the second quarter of the 19th century, but furnishing fabrics remained very shiny, as typified by the cottons in the Esther Cooper coverlet.

Chintz gradually came to describe large floral, highly glazed furnishing cottons, often with white backgrounds (the Esther Cooper coverlet's descriptive term in The Quilters' Guild Collection is 'Chintz Frame Coverlet'). The term 'chintzy' then referred to a flowery style of interior decoration and, by the 20th century, was used in a derogatory way – a far cry from the original meaning describing highly sought-after Indian cottons or complex block-printed fabrics.

Framed Taos by Annette Morgan, *96 x 96cm (38 x 38in)*

Red and White Basket Quilt, 202 x 244cm (79½ x 96in), late 19th or early 20th century

The striking Red and White Basket Quilt (opposite) gives us some clues about its origins. The quilting design was marked in blue pencil, the method traditionally used by north-country quilt markers or 'stampers' (see page 77). Combined with the style of the patchwork and the quilting patterns, this suggests that the quilt was made by a skilled quilter from the north east of England at the end of the 19th or beginning of the 20th century.[1] Measuring 202 x 244cm (79½ x 96in), the quilt is made in red and white cotton with alternating machine-pieced blocks of baskets and plain squares. The central blocks are surrounded by a wide, plain border with a basket block in each corner and the entire quilt is heavily hand quilted.

RED AND WHITE QUILT
JO REDNALL

The way the red baskets stood out on the Red and White Basket Quilt (opposite) inspired Jo Rednall to design Stepping Out (right) using the same highly contrasting colours. Her fascination for strong shapes and the potential of using counterchange and the Fibonacci series led to a bold, balanced design in stripes of varying widths.

'On quilts, I found that the Fibonacci stripe structure could be used in various, more complex ways.'

JO REDNALL

Jo started making quilts at evening class after seeing (and being intrigued by) a Log Cabin quilt at a church fair. Once retired from a career in computing, she spent four years working on the City and Guilds Patchwork and Quilting course. She acknowledges the help received from well-known quilter teachers. 'Deirdre Amsden taught me to hand quilt, use a thimble and use a spoon (!) to help in tacking (basting) the quilt sandwich together.' (Deirdre recommends using a spoon in the free hand to hold the quilt sandwich down immediately in front of where the next tacking (basting) stitch will be sewn – it stops the sandwich lifting up as the needle goes down and up through the layers.) 'Harriet Hargrave made me sit correctly at the sewing machine and opened my eyes a little further to the power of machine quilting.' (Harriet stresses that quilters should look down on their work when sewing, but many use too low a chair, which prevents this.)

When Jo first started making quilts she was drawn to traditional patterns, constantly recreating or absorbing the old patterns and trying to use them in some form. 'I was attracted to the idea of developing a contemporary red and white quilt.'

FIBONACCI – A DESIGN INFLUENCE

Jo became interested in the Fibonacci series of numbers whilst at college, where she used the series for ideas on the lines and forms of her designs. The series can be used to create a striped pattern with the widths of the stripes dictated by the numbers in the series. 'On quilts, I found that the Fibonacci stripe structure could be used in various, more complex ways. I could create stripes of widths that increased and decreased as I moved up and down the numerical series. And I could create numerous variations by cutting, rotating and re-joining the striped pieces.'

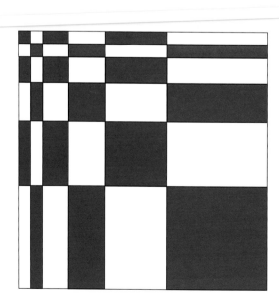

far left Diagram of the Fibonacci series represented as stripes

left Jo's design exercise using the Fibonacci series

Red and White Quilts

Detail of the Red and White Basket Quilt

The combination of red and white is frequently seen in quilts from the second half of the 19th and the early 20th century (see Sawtooth Strippy Quilt, page 98). At this time, many quilts were made by women who could not afford special fabric. They would recycle fabric and make use of fabric samples or factory 'fents' (a general term for ends of rolls, trial runs, misprints or damaged cloth). Often they were limited to the fabrics produced in large quantities for domestic and household purposes. Red and white quilts were made from white cotton generally with a plain (tabby) weave and red cotton called Turkey Red generally with a twill (diagonal) weave. A plain weave is worked when the weft thread goes over and under the warp thread in a regular pattern. A twill weave has the appearance of diagonal lines because the weft thread is worked over one and under two or more warp threads. White cotton was used extensively for bed linen and clothing, and late 19th-century drapers' catalogues show that Turkey Red cotton was sold widely in up to 12 fabric grades for making items such as children's clothing, underwear – and even the first bathing dresses.[2]

Striking quilt designs were achieved with the use of simple pieced or appliqué motifs (generally red motifs on a white background and only very rarely the reverse) and areas of plain cloth in the background were enhanced with detailed quilting. The basket motif was a block design typical of British quilts of the period and one that works particularly well where the colour contrast is high.

Quilters who stitched red and white quilts in the 19th century aimed to make pleasing but functional domestic textiles whilst working to a restricted budget. By the 20th century, when Turkey Red cotton production ended and red cotton became less fashionable for household textiles, the red and white combination became less used. Gradually (probably after the World War I), it came to represent 'blood and bandages', and was thought by some to bring bad luck. Superstitious nurses would not allow red and white flowers to be arranged together in hospital wards. Red and white would certainly not have been the colours of choice for a bedroom or a quilt. Fortunately, as these associations have passed, contemporary quilters are once again exploring the design possibilities of this colour combination.

THE FIBONACCI SERIES

Leonardo Pisano Fibonacci was born in 1170, probably in Pisa, Italy, and was educated in North Africa, where he was taught mathematics. He wrote a number of texts on mathematical topics that were influential in reviving an interest in ancient mathematical skills.

He developed a series of numbers in response to a mathematical problem that was posed concerning the number of rabbits produced in one year by a breeding pair and their offspring living in an enclosed space. Every number in the series is the sum of the two preceding numbers in the series, as follows: 1 1 2 3 5 8 13 21 34 55 89 144 and so on.

A visually pleasing series of stripes or a sequence of geometric shapes such as squares or rectangles can be created by using dimensions dictated by the numbers in the series. This is probably because the numbers in the series are in the same ratio as many proportions of growth found in nature such as the scales on a pine cone or the seeds at the centre of a coneflower (*Rudbeckia*) or sunflower (*Helianthus*).

Four painted sketches showing stages of the design development to demonstrate how counterchange alters at each stage

Diagram demonstrating counterchange

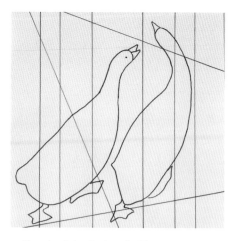

Sketch of the final grid of lines with the goose shapes added in the centre

CONTRAST AND SHAPES

In the Red and White Basket Quilt, Jo likes the way the red baskets stand out against the white background. This inspired her to seek out designs that work well with strongly contrasting colours. The alternate red and white triangles in the baskets give the effect of counterchange (a technique where the colours of a motif and its background are reversed in another part of the design). The quilt was 'the catalyst in making me place shapes on [a] Fibonacci series [a stripe design dictated by the Fibonacci series] – I had used both separately, but not together'.

Shapes fascinate Jo and many of her quilt designs evolve from paper cutouts, often after folding and cutting paper at random. It is no surprise that the artist Salvador Dali inspires her because many of the images in his paintings are shapes made up of shapes. Jo has used the traditional American appliqué design Noisy Geese[3] for a number of quilt projects. 'My plan was to use the Fibonacci series to create a red and white striped pattern on to which I would superimpose the Noisy Geese block. The addition of counterchange increased the complexity, creating a positive/negative effect by changing the positions of the red and white colours. The greater the number of components in the design, the more enhanced would be the effects of counterchange.'

MAKING THE DESIGN

Jo decided to make a quilt of just less than one metre (39in) square. 'I drew the design in stages on paper, working to the actual size, beginning with seven vertical stripes of variable width related to the Fibonacci series: 5, 3, 5, 8, 5, 3, 5. The stripe dimensions did not have to fit the Fibonacci numbers exactly, a little leeway does not harm the design.'

The Noisy Geese block design was scaled up to a size suitable for the dimensions of the quilt and placed on the stripes. Jo scaled up the geese until she was happy with the space they occupied in the centre of the striped background. An easy way of scaling up a picture is to use the enlarging facility on a photocopier. You can create a number of different sizes and experiment with them until you find one that fits the space well. The geese appeared to be walking uphill, so Jo added a path for them to walk on – a horizontal line sloping upwards. 'At this point I felt that the grid [made up of the six vertical lines and one horizontal] was taking on a life of its own and appeared to resemble woods: the vertical stripes had become tree trunks. I added two further lines slanting down from the top of the quilt to represent a shaft of light and to divide up the grid further. Then I included more woodland shapes of leaves, mushrooms and a woodpecker.'

Careful marking of the alternating red and white colours was required to achieve the counterchange effect. Starting at one edge of the top of the vertical stripes and working across the paper, Jo marked a colour change wherever the edge of a shape crossed a vertical stripe.

Noisy Geese Night and Day by Jo Rednall, 35.5 x 66 cm (14 x 26in)

Turkey Red

The bright Turkey Red cotton was created using a complex method of dyeing involving an alum mordant, which fixes the dye to the fibres of the cloth, and a red dye obtained from the madder plant or its synthesized component, alizarin. The bright colour was achieved by subjecting the cloth to a lengthy treatment with oils or fat before adding the mordant. This 'oiling' allows the mordant to unite well with the cotton fibres, thus producing a good dye result with the madder. The dyed cloth was then brightened in a bath of dissolved tin (stannous chloride). Until this process was discovered only a dull brown red could be obtained when dyeing cotton with madder and alum.[4]

The Turkey Red dye process was introduced into Europe from the Ottoman (Turkish) Empire in the 18th century. It was first used to dye thread, but European refinements of the process led to cloth dyeing. By the first quarter of the 19th century, discharge-printed Turkey Red cotton was produced in a process where areas of the red-dyed cloth were bleached white and colours such as black, blue and yellow were simultaneously overprinted on to the white. The production of Turkey Red cotton expanded through the 19th century, stimulating the growth of specialist dye works in England and Scotland, particularly in the Glasgow area. The cloth was used in Britain and exported extensively, particularly to India, the Far East, West Africa and South America. Interestingly, the Turkey Red cloth produced for the home market tended to be twill weave whilst export cloth was plain weave and often of a thinner quality.

Detail of a late 19th century frame quilt showing discharge-printed Turkey Red cotton

Sample for Geese Dreams showing organza
machine quilted on top of bonded shapes

Details of Stepping Out showing *top* hand
embroidered dandelion seed heads and
above machine quilting to give a sense
of dappled shade

CONSTRUCTION

White cotton was used to make the quilt. The red was obtained by dyeing the cloth using a cherry red washing machine dye. The colour subdivisions in some of the smaller shapes required a lot of fiddly piecing even though only two colours were being used, so Jo decided to use reverse appliqué to overcome this problem. In reverse appliqué, two or more fabric layers are assembled. Motifs are created by cutting away the shape required through the top layer to reveal the fabric below and then turning back and sewing down the raw edges of the top layer.

Jo pieced one grid design, without the added shapes of geese and woodland shapes, placing the colours as marked on her paper design. Then she made another grid design to serve as the under layer, with the colours reversed. The two layers were tacked (basted) together; then the shapes were marked on the top layer and stitched using reverse appliqué. The good quality cotton fabric was chosen partly because its tight, fine weave prevents the red areas of the lower layer showing through the white areas of the top layer.

'I machine quilted all over using a variety of coloured and metallic machine embroidery threads to give a sense of dappled shade in the woods. For further embellishment I added dandelion seed heads, hand embroidered in long stitch.'

Jo continued to pursue the red and white colour combination, creating another quilt in the Noisy Geese series – Geese Dreams. 'In this quilt I overcame the fiddly piecing problem, not with reverse appliqué but by bonding the fabric shapes to a base cloth of the stripes. I then laid organza over the whole top and machine quilted the entire quilt surface.'

Stepping Out by Jo Rednall, *84 x 88cm (33 x 35in)*

Late 19th-century Silk Log Cabin Table Cover, *122 x 120cm (48 x 47in)*, in silk, velvet and silk ribbon

The rich colours of this small quilt (opposite) draw the eye. Made from silks, velvets and ribbons, the Silk Log Cabin Table Cover was probably intended as a decorative item in a dining or sitting room. It was made towards the end of the 19th century and may have come from Scotland. The Table Cover is made from 100 blocks of Log Cabin patchwork in silk, silk ribbon and velvet in browns, reds, creams and blues, edged by a wide velvet border in rich terracotta brown. The blocks are made by sewing fabric strips around a central square and, in this Log Cabin variation, the darker strips are on two adjacent sides and the lighter strips on the other two sides, giving a diagonal contrast across the blocks.

LOG CABIN QUILT
DINAH TRAVIS

Dinah Travis was inspired by the many different fabrics in the Log Cabin Table Cover (opposite) to use unusual silk prints from her stash for Cross-hatch (right). Departing from the idea of having to make a Log Cabin quilt, she realized that she could still portray that feel with a diagonal furrow pattern. The central strips are left free to fray at the edges.

DINAH TRAVIS

The women in Dinah's family were all active needlewomen or craftspeople; there were even Welsh quilts on the beds. Art school trained, it was natural for her to follow the same textile route and 'sewing was easier than oil painting when my young children were around'. She has been making quilts since 1978, led by her childhood memories of bed quilts and she finds inspiration in the painterly qualities of the quilts of Deirdre Amsden.

Dinah has been a leading quilt teacher for over 20 years for City and Guilds and, with fellow quilt teacher Pat Salt, on her own international correspondence course. Log Cabin patchwork was her first focus, but her interest soon widened. She has made traditional quilts to demonstrate design and techniques, and has published books on sampler, appliqué and miniature quilts.[1,2,3] Her quilts are widely exhibited in national quilt exhibitions.

'My own technique has been developed from the need to express ideas in a practical way. All my quilts look quite fragile but will stand up to the rigours of machine washing. I use the rich features of both silk and cotton fabrics intended for fashion or furnishing. Silk pieces are secured by a stitched grid to a cotton base with the edges left free to fray. My designs are simple in concept, with the play of one colour against another, with repeating patterns being an important feature'.

'My designs are simple in concept … with repeating patterns being an important feature.'

From Start to Finish by Dinah Travis,
100 x 100cm (39 x 39in)

Log Cabin and its Origins

Log Cabin patchwork has been a popular technique since the second half of the 19th century, but in their book *Making Connections Around the World with Log Cabin*, Janet Rae and Dinah Travis highlight the obscurity of its origins. They show similar patterns used in weaving, embroidery, wrappings, mosaics and other ornamentation, including a Log Cabin embroidery pattern seen on stumpwork boxes of the 17th century, but they are unable to demonstrate a direct link.[4] In the middle of the 19th century pattern and ornamentation were closely influenced by classical design and patterns published in a number of design books such as *Grammar of Ornament* of 1856. Such books were influential in popularizing geometric pattern sourced from history and they could have been responsible for acquainting needlewomen with the design,[5] especially as the oldest surviving Log Cabin quilts date from 1850–60.

The traditional way of making a Log Cabin block is to sew fabric strips on to a foundation cloth, rotating the strips around a central square. The strips are either seamed down to the foundation and then flipped over to cover the seam line or folded before tacking (basting) to the foundation with the raw edges covered by the overlapping strip on the next row. The pattern is highly suitable for a wide variety of fabrics because it relies on the effective use of tonal values rather than exact matching of colours or printed patterns.

The tonal contrast between dark and light strips in Log Cabin patchwork is exploited when the blocks are joined together; the blocks can be repeated with the same orientation across the quilt or rotated to create a variety of different layout patterns. In the Silk Log Cabin Table Cover (see page 46), rotating alternate blocks through 180 degrees creates strong diagonal stripes across the piece. The late 19th-century cotton Log Cabin coverlet (below) has the blocks orientated so that the dark sides are together.

During the 19th century, needlewomen from different social classes exploited the Log Cabin pattern, working it in distinctly different styles. Frugal needlewomen in straitened circumstances made utilitarian quilts by recycling household textiles and resorting to cotton, linen and wool fents and samples in a wide variety of colours and print, as typified by the cotton Log Cabin coverlet below. Towards the end of the 19th century this technique was used with silks, ribbons and velvets for more decorative patchwork and was widely mentioned in needlework books, where it was called variously American Log patchwork, Canadian or Loghouse patchwork, Egyptian or Mummy pattern (referring back to ancient wrapping patterns for Egyptian mummies) and Roof pattern. The name Log Cabin has been connected to Abraham Lincoln's 1864 US presidential campaign, but the pattern itself predates this time.[6]

These more showy Log Cabin pieces were often decorated with additional embroidered embellishment as seen in the detail of the Jubilee Quilt (page 52). This quilt uses an unusual Log Cabin method to create the central petals of the flowers by alternating two colours of strips. This unique design was recorded twice during the British Quilt Heritage Project.

Cotton Log Cabin coverlet, *190 x 221cm (75 x 87in)*, late 19th century

Dinah's quilt From Start to Finish (see page 48) was the first in a series of quilts based on mazes and Log Cabin blocks. It was made with silk applied to a cotton foundation, frayed and machine stitched to a backing.

INSPIRED BY FABRIC

Dinah has been working with the Log Cabin pattern for some years and initially she had 'no spark of inspiration except to produce yet another Log Cabin quilt!' She usually starts by scribbling with a pen and squared paper to establish a pattern idea and layout, then moving to painting and free drawing. However, this project was different. 'I turned to the fabric and the colour for an idea. The Silk Log Cabin Table Cover suggested the use of many different fabrics, which suited me, as my collection of fabrics consisted of a wide range of small and large pieces of silk fabrics in both plains and prints. These were collected over the years from various sources, [some] dating back to my mother's heyday of dressmaking in the 1920s, remnants gathered from a silk factory in South East London, a collection of dupion silks and donations from friends and neighbours who just left their scraps on my doorstep because they could not bear to throw them away.'

Dinah does not use fabric that is specifically produced for quilters, preferring more unusual materials or plain cloth that she can dye and mark herself. She started with the colours from the Silk Log Cabin Table Cover, 'sorting through what many quilters would think of as a pile of rubbish (no pile of fat quarters for me)'. She selected light colours with a hint of blue and darker tones in a range of warm browns, instinctively selecting a wide

Fabrics from Dinah's stash

Pages from Dinah's sketchbook: diagonals and colours

Pages from Dinah's sketchbook: experiments with borders

range of colours 'reflecting everyday life'. Having arranged the fabric in the order in which they might be used, Dinah could begin thinking about the quilt.

IMPRESSIONS OF THE TABLE COVER

An early decision was to make the project quilt square, so Dinah made many scribbled drawings of Log Cabin quilts in this shape, always returning to the diagonal furrow-like look created by the way the blocks were assembled. She liked the idea of a wide border and looked at the proportions of different widths. 'It took me some time to realize that I did not have to make a Log Cabin quilt to portray the feel of the Silk Log Cabin Table Cover. The diagonal element of the furrow pattern repeatedly kept coming into mind. I made lots of rough paintings of diagonals in blues and browns. I cut them up and gave them various borders. I liked the way the diagonals were coming out on to the border in some of these designs, but felt that the diagonals were becoming too dominant.' Concerned that this would cause a technical problem when she started to sew, she made a small fabric sample to work out how the quilt would be made – 'a simple and practical step' that is often missed, with the result that a quilt can become too complex.

'The sample allowed me to decide on a size of the quilt and how I would apply and piece the fabrics.' Dinah's quilt would be made up of a central square of freely applied strips chosen from the silk prints in her fabric pile and running diagonally from top left to bottom right. The wide border was to be made up of larger pieces of plain silks continuing the diagonal out to the edge in a more subdued range of colours.

Pages from Dinah's sketchbook: blue and brown diagonals and borders

Pages from Dinah's sketchbook: more diagonals and borders

Final design and colouring

Centre detail of Jubilee Quilt (see page 72) made by Mrs Mills in 1887 – the 'flowers' are made by exploiting the tonal contrast seen in Log Cabin patchwork to create bi-coloured petals

MAKING THE QUILT

The strips of the central square were machine sewn on to a cotton square, each overlapping with the edges left free to fray. The border was backed with cotton to balance the weight of the central square and joined to it with a flat seam. The whole quilt was then backed with a cotton square. 'At this stage, I felt that the division between centre and border needed more definition so silk strips were placed round the central square and the edge to act as a narrow border.'

Dinah did more sketches to help make the decision on how to quilt the border. 'To counteract the diagonal, I planned to hand "tack" (baste) quilt the border in columns. The idea of using a large stitch for quilting and a variety of threads came from tacking (basting) together many quilts over the years and being attracted to the way the tacking (basting) stitch was making layers on to one fabric.' She worked diagonally across the quilt following the strips using a wide stitch of roughly uniform length and spacing and various coloured threads, blue tones against the reds and browns and vice versa. The even stitching had the effect of creating raised ridges that ran across the diagonals in the opposite direction.

Dinah considered several ideas for a name for her contemporary quilt around the word 'furrow' such as ploughed, sand ripple, strata, corrugated silk and ribbed. 'Finally Cross-hatch, which means to hatch a surface with crossing sets of parallel lines, was chosen.'

Detail of Cross-hatch

Cross-hatch by Dinah Travis, *91 x 90.5cm (36 x 35½in)*

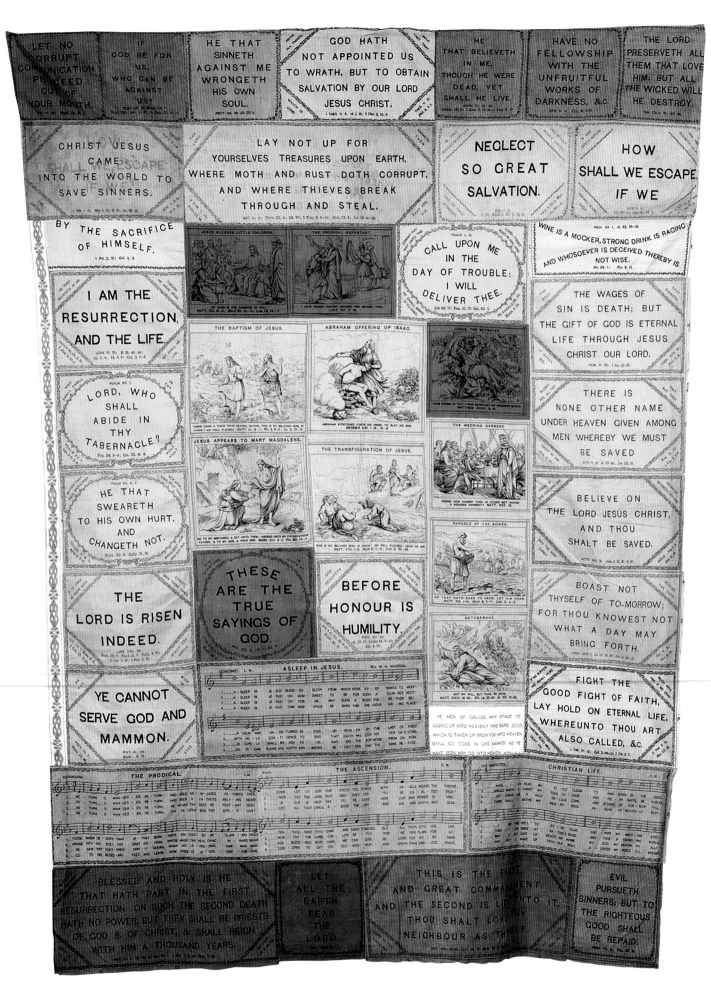

Bible Coverlet, *115 x 161cm (45 x 63in),* made some time after 1876

The maker of this small, unusual coverlet (opposite) was possibly from Spennymoor, County Durham, northern England, but her identity is less important than the very specific message she conveys. The Bible Coverlet consists of a number of square and rectangular printed cotton blocks containing scripture quotations, religious music and finely engraved biblical scenes. It was clearly intended to set an example of Christian belief and provide inspiration to anyone who used it. The coverlet was pieced very simply, some time after 1876, with apparently little thought to symmetry or colour balance in the arrangement of the blocks. It was originally loosely backed with a coarse wool fabric, now removed.

QUILT WITH A MESSAGE
HILARY RICHARDSON

The Bible Coverlet (opposite) inspired Hilary Richardson to create Rural Rape (right), her quilt with a message. She developed her ideas by researching dictionary definitions of related words, and collecting photographs, cuttings and printed material. The images were scanned and printed using three different computer-aided techniques.

HILARY RICHARDSON

Hilary is both a potter and a quilter. She divides her time between these two contrasting hard and soft crafts, making domestic and commemorative pottery as well as quilts, and teaching patchwork from beginner's level to City and Guilds. She cannot remember a time when she could not sew, knit and crochet; she took up quilting in 1987 because she was drawn to the challenge of its 'precision and geometry'. Hilary tends to use machine quilting techniques because of past medical problems (now cured), but she plans to use more hand sewing methods in the future. Fabric dyeing and printing feature strongly in her work, as do computer-based printing techniques.

Various aspects of her personal life have recently come into Hilary's quilts. Two of them featured feet and shoes because she has unusually small feet. Other ideas revolve around transport and farming issues, and the way people are affected by the activities of nearby farms. She was involved in a court case after she and four other beekeepers lost their bees when a local farmer sprayed an oilseed rape (*Brassica napus*) crop.

'The [Bible Coverlet] design itself is simple, but you cannot ignore the messages.'

Hilary finds a connection with the instigator of the printed scripture blocks, who had 'the courage to have the blocks made because of his own strong beliefs'. Using the techniques already tried in her quilt Shoes (left), she decided to make a quilt to show her feelings about some modern farming practices.

MESSAGES AND ADVERTISING

It is not only religious messages that can be found in patchwork and quilting. Many people have found that simple domestic textiles are a good way of raising funds, supporting a campaign or even promoting a product.

From the end of the 19th century until the 1930s, printed and woven cigarette silks and tobacco flannels were produced as incentives to purchase particular tobacco brands. They were supplied in cigarette packets, wrapped around purchases, or in return for a coupon received with the tobacco. Produced in both Britain and North America, they were aimed at children and needlewomen, even though men consumed most of the tobacco.[1] The manufacturers were able to encourage brand loyalty by tapping into a craze for collecting these silks and promoting the fashion for using them in numerous fancy articles such as cushions (pillows), lingerie cases and tea cosies, such as the one made from printed silks shown far right.[2]

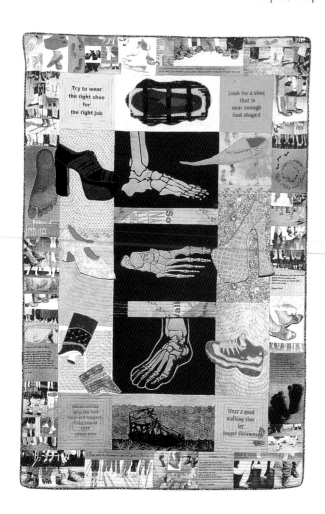

Shoes by Hilary Richardson, *78 x 119cm (31 x 47in)*

Printed Scripture Blocks

Detail of the Bible Coverlet

Only eight quilts and coverlets with printed scripture blocks in the style of those seen in the Bible Coverlet have been identified.[3] The blocks were the work of a Victorian evangelist, Robert Mimpriss, who was inspired to use simple domestic textiles to convey a message of religious conviction to devout families and residents in public institutions such as reformatories, workhouses and hospitals. Although his health was poor, Mimpriss devoted time to designing a series of blocks using suitable religious texts, music and pictures; 126 different blocks have been identified in the eight recorded quilts and coverlets alone.[4] The engraved designs were printed in Crayford, Kent on to cotton fabric of various colours.

After Robert Mimpriss's death in 1876, his widow's agent took over the project and sold the designs in sets of blocks or as made-up quilts. Each block has a number or letter in the seam allowance – a possible guide to the order of joining the blocks and suggesting a very early quilt kit. The sets and quilts were promoted in a temperance magazine called *The British Workman*, but it is unknown how else they were advertised. Three of the coverlets have known Methodist connections and it is documented that chapel sewing groups made up two others.

Many contemporary quilters also use their work to convey feelings and opinions about current issues. Hilary Richardson is one of them. Another such quilter, Michelle Walker says, 'I aim in my work to challenge the association of the word "quilt".' She believes 'it is essential that the content of the work should reflect the time in which it is made'.[5] Her small quilt, House Block, in The Quilters' Guild Nineties Collection was the second quilt she made in response to graffiti about the

Cigarette silks tea cosy, 1915

House Block by Michele Walker, 60.5 x 61cm (24 x 24in)

homeless in Brighton, West Sussex – 'No home, No vote, No job, No chance'. She used plastic material such as bin liners, carrier bags, newspaper and assorted threads and buttons with hand-stencilled lettering.

PREPARING THE MESSAGE

When Hilary begins a quilt on a specific theme, she seeks clues in the dictionary definitions of words connected to the theme. She will often make a list of words and topics that

Collected cuttings and images on the theme

Hilary's photo of work in progress
on the design wall

relate to the theme. She then collects photographs, cuttings and printed material, and finds the Internet useful for researching topics.

For this quilt, Hilary had plenty of cuttings relating to her successful court case, to which she added recent articles on oilseed rape farming, GM rape experiments, beekeepers' reference material and many photographs of bees and oilseed rape plants. This research and preparation stage could be used for a design on any topic. Hilary feels that the time spent collecting the material can also be used to think about how the cuttings and images will work when brought together in a quilt.

Though she may start with a rough idea of how the quilt will look, Hilary expects it to change and develop. She often draws a sketch to show the size and shape of the quilt, and the positions of some of the researched material. However, for her the main design stage is when she starts to arrange her material, adding to it as her quilt design grows. Quilters who design organically often find that using a large area of wall is very useful; the design material can be fixed to it, rearranged and then left for further reassessment. Hilary's design wall is a pinboard covered with a flannelette sheet, but you could hang a sheet down from the top of a wall and pin to that.

ALLOWING THE DESIGN TO GROW

An early decision was to make the quilt rectangular, landscape style, with the centre in a brown frame that has the proportions of a beehive's brood frame (this type of frame is a structure on which the bees build a honeycomb, in this case a honeycomb for the developing young bees). As the layout developed, Hilary transferred the chosen photographs and printed material from paper to cloth, using three different fabric-printing techniques to get the right effect. Two of the techniques were entirely computer based, which restricted the images to A4 (21 x 29.7cm / 8¼ x 11¾in), as that was the largest size of paper her printer would take. This restriction had an effect on the final size of the quilt.

COMPUTER PRINTING ON FABRIC

The first stage was to scan photographs and newspaper cuttings into the computer and print them on to cotton fabric using a computer product called Bubble Jet Set (see page 87 for instructions on computer printing on to fabric).

The printed scripture blocks in the Bible Coverlet were printed generally in black on coloured cotton with a fine engraved border surrounding a central text. Hilary created her own blocks in this style using CorelDraw software. Their content was made up of quotations from her court judgment, descriptions of honeybees and chemical formulae of herbicides and insecticides used on oilseed

Image on paper and computer-printed fabric

rape crops, all in a variety of fonts. These were then edged with borders of leaves, flowers and bees. Hilary computer printed these on to coloured cotton that she had dyed with cold-water fibre reactive dyes.

TRANSFER PRINTS

The brightly coloured biohazard chemicals and 'no bees' warning signs, together with the *Chichester Observer* logo, were printed using a transfer printing technique.

To make the honeycomb for the two central corners of the quilt, Hilary hand pieced individual hexagons from white cotton over paper templates. She created transfer prints of hexagons in oranges and yellows, some containing images of the developing bee, and ironed them on to the white hexagons.

Block design and computer-printed fabric

MAKING A TRANSFER PRINT

This method is very effective for images that require a strong colour but will make the fabric stiffer than computer-printed fabric. The images to use for transfer printing are either computer generated or scanned into the computer.

METHOD

1. Use the drawing software to flip the chosen design horizontally so that the design appears to be the wrong way round (later, the transfer process will reverse this back again so that it is the right way round).

2. Check the printer settings options and change to 'T shirt transfers'. Print the flipped block on to computer transfer paper.

3. Check the instructions of the specific product you are using and then iron the transfer on to cotton.

BLUEPRINTS (CYANOTYPES)

Blueprinting is a long-used photographic technique that creates white on blue prints. The white print develops when areas of sensitized paper or cloth are shielded from light whilst the rest of the exposed paper or cloth turns blue. Hilary uses the method to print on to cloth from negatives, which she produces on the computer and also to obtain silhouettes of objects such as plant material by laying them straight on to cloth to make a mask before exposing the cloth to light.

The blueprinted words on the top and bottom borders of the quilt were created using CorelDraw software. The words were typed on to a white filled rectangle

Image, negative and cyanotype

BLUEPRINTING

The cloth requires sensitization in a photographic dark room and the process involves the use of chemicals. Block out all natural light and illuminate the room with a 'safe light' (red covered light bulb). Ensure that the room is ventilated and wear protective clothing, rubber gloves and a face mask. Keep the containers used for the process separate, label the chemicals and the mixed solutions clearly and store them safely.

YOU WILL NEED

60g (2oz) ferric ammonium citrate

30g (1oz) potassium ferricyanide

500ml (16oz or 2 cups) water

Large shallow tray, such as a cat litter tray

Perspex or glass large enough to cover both the negative or the chosen object and the cotton fabric

Rigid board larger than the fabric

Cotton fabric (washed and ironed)

METHOD

1. Dissolve the ferric ammonium citrate in 250ml (8oz or 1 cup) water. Dissolve the potassium ferricyanide in the rest of the water.
2. In the dark room with the safe light on, mix the two solutions in the shallow tray.
3. Soak the fabric in the mixed solution and hang it to dry in the dark room. Store the remaining solution in brown glass jars for further fabric treatment.
4. Iron the dry fabric in the dark room, place it in two black plastic bags (one bag inside the other) and store it out of the light in a box or drawer.
5. Choose a sunny day for the blueprinting. Put the fabric on the rigid board with a negative or plant material on top and cover with Perspex or glass.
6. Place the covered fabric and board in the sun. The exposure can be from about 5 to 20 minutes depending on the season and the strength of the light, so tests should be done for the right exposure time. If the sun is at a lower angle in the winter, the board should be tilted towards the sun.
7. When the fabric has been exposed, wash it immediately until the rinse water is clear.
8. Dry the fabric. It can then be ironed before use. The print becomes clear and darkens as the fabric dries.

Hilary's photo of blueprinting the rape plant in the sun

and then the 'invert' command was used to turn the words white and the background black. Hilary changed the printer properties/paper setting to 'transparency film' and printed on to computer transparency paper (in this case using three sheets with a little overlap). The three sheets were trimmed and clear taped together to make one long strip of negative, which was used to print on to the fabric. The blueprints on the side borders were created using self-sown rape plants found on the roadside as masks for printing.

THE DESIGN BECOMES THE QUILT

When creating a design, Hilary transfers all the chosen paper designs on to fabric and positions the fabric pieces on her wall until she is satisfied with the design and has an almost finished layout. At this point she makes decisions about how any remaining areas of the design will be treated. In Rural Rape, she wanted the centre section of the quilt to be filled with a rape plant in flower. She cut the plant shape from yellow and green cotton and then bonded it, using a fusible web (such as Bondaweb), on to a blue cotton background that had been transfer printed with an oilseed rape flower head. The brown frame around the centre section has added horizontal lugs (as seen on frames in beehives) with green spacers (the colour chosen to designate the 2004 beekeeping season) running into the border.

The design components were machine pieced, following the layout on the wall. Once the piecing was complete, extra

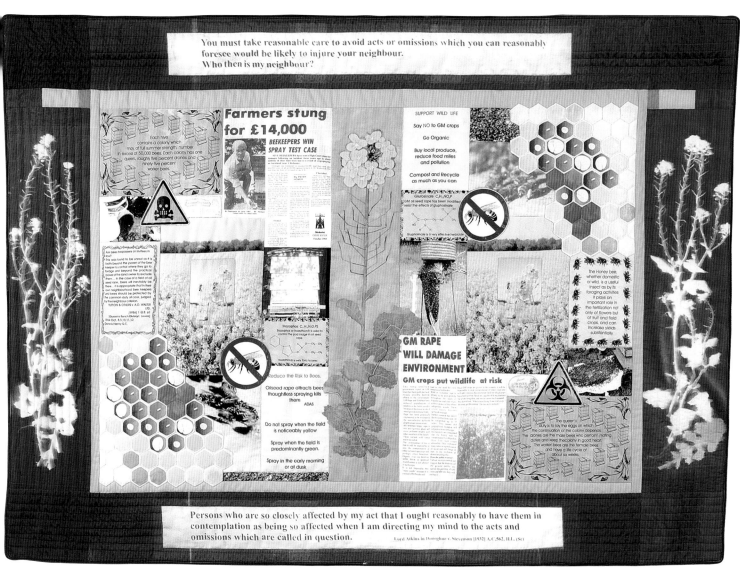

Rural Rape by Hilary Richardson, 92.5 x 128cm (36½ x 50in)

leaves were added to the applied oilseed rape plant, passing across the seams on to adjacent printed blocks. Individual yellow rape flowers were sewn on to the blue background, leaving the edges of the petals free to give a three-dimensional effect. The flowers were embellished with free machine embroidery to create the seed heads and small stalks.

When it came to quilting the piece, Hilary chose to stitch by machine, outlining the blocks and adding rows of lines along the border. The edge was finished with piping. Hilary named her quilt Rural Rape, taking two meanings from the common name for *Brassica napus*.

Happy that her quilt is following the tradition of the Bible Coverlet, she said 'They [Robert Mimpriss and the makers] can have had no idea of the effect these quilts would have, if any, but still did it. The quilt design itself is very simple but you cannot ignore the messages'.

Detail of Rural Rape

Damascus Coat, 19th century

This striking coat (opposite) was probably brought from the Middle East to Britain as a souvenir. Made sometime during the 19th century, it is a typical example of the type of informal coat often made in the Damascus area. Loose overgarments like this would have been worn for relaxed occasions such as gatherings at the bathhouse.[1] The coat shape is simple – square-set sleeves, side slits instead of pockets and no fastenings on the front. Corded quilting creates the interesting surface texture; two layers of fabric are joined by hand-sewn channels down which cotton cords are threaded from the back. The pattern down the front edges and centre back, and along the hem, is made from diagonal and zigzag lines of cording, interspersed with a four-petal floral motif in the body of the coat.

CORD-QUILTED CUSHION
JUDY FAIRLESS

Judy Fairless was fascinated with the play of light on the ridges created by the straight lines of corded quilting on the Damascus Coat (opposite). She could see new possibilities of developing a similar effect in chamois leather. So, experimenting with corrugated paper, she created her Chamois Leather Cushion, a modern design just asking to be touched.

JUDY FAIRLESS

A Quilters' Guild national exhibition in the early 1980s was Judy's first introduction to quilting. Trained as a primary school teacher, she applied her childhood sewing skills first to embroidery, then quilting and she now teaches the City and Guilds Patchwork and Quilting course. Judy has developed a reputation for elegant quilt designs, often with subdued colouring.

Judy likes to mix the two crafts of embroidery and quilting, using many different machine piecing and quilting techniques. Currently, she says, 'I am having a "thing" working with chamois (chammy) leather. My experiments with machine quilting on leather resulted in interesting effects enhanced by the grain of the skin, so I want to develop this technique – the only thing holding me back is the difficulty of getting the leather in large enough pieces.' This is not a new problem. A needlework dictionary for 1882 features kid patchwork, 'this patchwork is generally confined to the making of such small articles as pincushions, slippers or mats, as the kid generally used for the purpose is cut from old gloves, and therefore is not of a large size; but if the pieces can be obtained of sufficient size cushions (pillows), footstools and other large articles may be attempted'.[2] Judy's quilt No Kidding is an updated wholecloth quilt inspired by a study of shoes, worked in chamois leather with the sections joined by long bootlaces.

Judy keeps a number of notebooks on various design themes and is constantly adding to them. She studies a design source, pattern or motif and reproduces it by drawing, printing or paper cutting. Using tried and trusted design methods, she will then play with the motifs by creating pattern repeats, rotating and mirror imaging the design. Her books are filled with pages of patterns reproduced in many ways, from plain lead pencil to vibrant colour – all waiting to provide inspiration for future work.

'I am having a "thing" working with chamois (chammy) leather.'

No Kidding by Judy Fairless,
91 x 124cm (39 x 49in)

THE FASCINATION WITH CORDED QUILTING

Corded quilting is very much an 18th-century technique; items of 19th-century work in Britain are rare. In the early 1920s and 1930s there was a revival of interest in the technique amongst amateur embroiderers. Renamed Italian quilting, it was used for decoration on small objects such as cushions (pillows) and sachets, and for the centres of feather-filled eiderdowns, often worked in fine silk or even one of the early synthetic silks.

Contemporary quilters are exploring the potential of the method. Helen Parrott made a series of quilts using corded and stuffed quilting, inspired by the ancient cup-and-ring markings seen on the Yorkshire Moors. Her small quilt, Ilkley Moor 1981 (top right) in The Quilters' Guild Nineties Collection, is part of this series.

18th-century baby's cap
using corded quilting on linen

Judy is fascinated by corded quilting and especially its ridges. 'For this project, I saw new possibilities in working corded quilting on leather. I studied the traditional motifs seen in 18th-century cord-quilted garments such as the baby's cap (below left), then experimented with the flower and leaf motifs in my sketchbook.' Gathering the patterns together, she sketched some possible uses for the designs on small caps and bags. Using one of the floral designs, she worked a sample of corded quilting in tan brown mock suede, sewing the channels by machine. She decided that the resulting patterns, though attractive, were not sufficiently innovative and the curves were awkward to machine sew.

FROM CURVES TO LINES

Judy was increasingly drawn to the straight-line patterns on the baby's cap (below left) and the Damascus Coat. 'I decided to abandon the curves of the floral designs for the jagged zigzag effects of the lines and went "back to the drawing board" to experiment with more patterns.'

Pieces of corrugated paper were useful in representing the relief effect of lines of corded quilting. Large-scale corrugated paper was stuck down in patterns with squares and triangles of paper to study the play of light and shade across the ridges. The resulting patterns were best suited to a square design, ideal for a small item such as a cushion (pillow).'

Judy experimented with a variation of corded quilting by inserting cords into channels from the top surface, leaving the ends showing. Unwittingly, she was referring back to earlier decorative techniques using cords. In the 18th century, men's

Ilkley Moor 1981 by Helen Parrott, 61 x 61.5cm (24 x 24in)

cord-quilted waistcoats often incorporated pulled-thread or embroidered infillings with surface applied cords in an imitation of lace. A pair of embroidered silk sleeves from the 17th century in the Victoria and Albert Museum, London, has 'S' lengths of satin-covered cotton cord couched down on to the silk surface in a wave pattern grid.[3]

The worked leather samples helped Judy to decide her final design. She created the surface cording by applying a patch of leather on to the top surface and sewing channels across it. This looked best if space was left between the blocks of cording. 'I found that diagonally sewn channels distorted the leather. I liked the contrast of a brown cord (shoelaces) with the cream leather, so I left the ends of the cords as tufts.'

Impressions of floral motifs taken from two babies' caps: in paint, ink and string

Half-floral motif used as border patterns

Corded Quilting in Clothing

Corded quilting gives textural pattern and body to a fabric without the warmth-giving layer of wadded quilting, but it is very labour intensive because making the hand-sewn channels for the cording, and threading the cords neatly from the back, takes a long time. There are many surviving 18th-century examples of bed coverings and clothing made from corded quilting. At this time, quilted garments were an important part of men's and women's wardrobes, and corded quilting was frequently used for men's waistcoats, women's jackets, formal and informal gowns, as well as babies' gowns and caps.[4] There was a flourishing trade in professionally made wadded and cord-quilted clothes, ready-made and to order (the latter with greater variety in design). The waistcoats were often sold as uncut panels, to be made up to fit the purchaser.[5,6] The handwork on cord-quilted garments was expensive, so this

Baby's cap – corded quilting on linen with pulled work and French knots, 18th century

was clothing for the wealthy, but it was also more practical being easier to launder than the fashionable fancy woven silk fabrics.

There was a long-established hand quilting industry based around the area of Marseilles, southern France, so items of corded quilting or *broderie de Marseille* made in white cotton were widely known across Europe during the 17th and 18th centuries.[7] French bedcovers worked entirely in corded quilting were highly sought after, at a price, since they would have taken many hundreds of hours to make. *Broderie de Marseille* was imported into Britain, but there was also a thriving domestic quilting industry. Trade cards from 18th-century businesses in London advertised both wadded and 'French' quilting, the latter term referring to corded quilting. English ladies who could not afford the imported French goods could purchase locally made items as well as the marked cloths and cotton cords to work the corded quilting themselves.[8]

Line patterns from the Damascus Coat using corrugated paper

Designing using corrugated paper

Final design for the cushion (pillow), in paper, corrugated card and wool

Line patterns

A LEATHER CUSHION

Judy created a mock-up for the final design for the cushion (pillow) using brown and white paper, corrugated card and cream wool. The centre was to be surface cord quilted, with a wide straight edge to the cushion in standard corded quilting, where the cording would be hidden on the back.

With the design transferred to tracing paper, Judy machine stitched the channel design for the border through the paper on to the leather top, which was backed with cotton fabric. She applied square patches of leather for the surface cording and stitched channels for cording with the brown shoelaces. The back of the cushion (pillow) was decorated with a panel of surface cording and a feature was made of the opening by adding metal eyelets and brown cord lacing.

All the sewing was done using a machine needle for leather. 'A walking foot was useful for all the straight sewing and I sewed the surface corded squares using a zipper foot.'

FINAL RESULT

Judy plans to continue her 'thing with chammy leather'. She said: 'I like the tactile feel of the leather. When it is combined with the textural designs of corded quilting, it is just asking to be touched.'

above Chamois Leather Cushion by Judy Fairless, 50 x 50cm (19¾ x 19¾in)

left Back of Chamois Leather Cushion with surface cording, eyelets and lacing

Flower Tea Cosy, *36.5 x 23.5cm (14 x 9in)*, early 20th century

This undeniably charming tea cosy (opposite) is only 23.5cm (9in) high, but it is made from many irregular patches of silk and velvet, each heavily embellished with delightful floral and decorative embroidery. Made at the beginning of the 20th century, the Flower Tea Cosy was found in a charity shop and donated to The Quilters' Guild in 1992. It is a fine example of Crazy patchwork, which is usually found on larger covers, throws, cushions (pillows) or coverlets, such as the Irish Crazy Patchwork Coverlet (page 71) made in 1880 by Elizabeth Ferguson.

CRAZY QUILT
LINDA KEMSHALL

The random shapes of the Flower Tea Cosy (opposite) reminded Linda Kemshall of the fragmented nature of mosaics and parched desert landscapes. She hand dyed and painted fabrics to give subtle colour changes, broken by a strong fracture line across her quilt, Fracture (right). A simplified grass shape, worked in hand and machine stitching provides a strong connection to the traditions of Crazy patchwork.

LINDA KEMSHALL

Linda claims that she came to textiles by a circuitous route. Trained as a painter and having sewn from childhood, she was introduced to quiltmaking when she worked with a colleague who made patchwork in her tea break. The hobby soon developed into a full time activity after Linda took the City and Guilds Patchwork and Quilting course, achieving their Medal of Excellence in 1995. Linda has taught City and Guilds courses in the UK and the USA and, since 2001, online. She is now an external verifier and National Advisor for the City and Guilds Patchwork and Quilting course.

Linda loves colouring cloth and is very comfortable with all the fabric painting and dyeing techniques. 'With the wealth of products available now, I can achieve the painted effects on fabric that I have so long loved on paper.' The quilters she admires most, like Michael James, Nancy Crow and Erika Carter, are similarly able to colour, paint and print cloth to stunning effect. Linda's book *Colour Moves – Transfer Paints on Fabric* was published in 2001.[1] Linda is well known for her very painterly quilts, many of the early pieces being figurative, as seen in her quilt Demons in My Head (below) for The Quilters' Guild Nineties Collection. A continuing theme has been feathers, angels and birds; some of her most striking quilts have featured the crows often seen around her south Staffordshire home.

'I can [now] achieve the painted effects on fabric that I have so long loved on paper.'

above Pages from Linda's sketchbook: detail of the Flower Tea Cosy with patterns from the stitches

INSPIRATIONS

Linda's painter's eye is always open for interesting designs, patterns and colours – constantly seeking new images to explore. Working with oil pastel and watercolour, she fills her sketchbooks with landscapes, rock formations and architecture as well as birds and feathers. For this project, she started with images of the Flower Tea Cosy and then added her impressions of the randomly shaped, coloured cloth and the embroidery stitches.

Linda often begins a design by brainstorming words and phrases. 'I was drawn to the fragmented nature of the Crazy patchwork and saw connections both with mosaics (such as those in the buildings designed by Antonio Gaudi in Barcelona) and parched desert landscapes. I studied the "crazy" nature of these two diverse themes, and painted and drew images in my sketchbook. The fragments in the images led me to the idea of fractures, so I experimented by cutting apart segments and rejoining them, often with staples. I also admired the embroidery in the tea cosy, especially the shaded colours of the flowers and leaves, so I added a simplified version of a grass shape to my drawings and this motif became a strong feature in the design.'

Demons in My Head, *60 x 61cm (23½ x 24in)*, by Linda Kemshall, made for the Nineties Collection in 1997

Crazy Patchwork

Crazy patchwork, very popular during the late 19th and early 20th century, was usually worked in luxury fabrics such as silks and velvets to create decorative items not intended for heavy use. It has been suggested that Crazy patchwork was inspired by the Japanese textiles seen in the exhibitions held in Europe and the USA during the second half of the 19th century, a time when Japanese decorative arts captured the imagination of the western world.[2,3] Crazy patchwork was soon mentioned in needlework books alongside embroidery and in 1882, it was featured as Puzzle patchwork in a British dictionary of needlework.[4]

In Crazy patchwork, randomly shaped fabric pieces are laid on to a foundation cloth, each piece overlapped on one edge by the adjacent piece. Once tacked (basted) to the foundation, the pieces are attached by embroidery stitches along the edges of the pieces, which also neatens them. At its simplest, the embroidery may be herringbone or feather stitch, but heavy embellishment is seen on many items from this period.

Canadian Red Cross quilts, which were brought into the UK in great quantities during World War II (see page 24), were often made using Crazy patchwork. Because these were utilitarian quilts they were not heavily embellished.

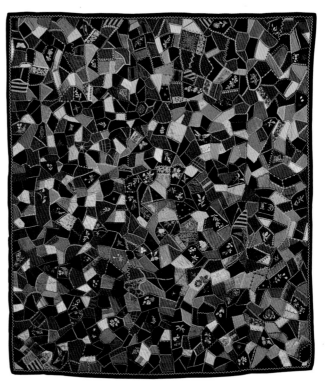

Irish Crazy Patchwork Coverlet, *208 x 229cm (82 x 90in)*, made by Elizabeth Ferguson in 1880 using silks and velvets

PUTTING THE IDEAS INTO THE QUILT

Linda likes Crazy patchwork because it is 'an ideal method for free appliqué designs with a painterly sense of colour'. To bring together elements of Victorian Crazy patchwork with Gaudi's distressed mosaic surfaces and images from deserts, she chose a random shape with washes of colour. 'Crazy patchwork was usually worked with contrasting colours so that the shapes stood out, but I wanted the colour changes to be far subtler so that the shapes gradually become apparent when the quilt is viewed more closely. Starting with pale desert colours at the top of the quilt, the colour would become darker and change downwards to deeper blues, reds, greens and purples drawn from Gaudi's mosaics. I wanted the colour change to be emphasized by a strong fracture running diagonally across the quilt, the two parts connected by beads, which would also be added as final embellishments across the quilt.' (Many of Linda's recent quilts have been made in segments linked with cords or beads.)

Pages from Linda's sketchbook: *above* showing impressions of a parched desert landscape and *below* showing images of fragments and fractures cut and stapled together with added grass seed heads

Embellishment on Quilts

At certain stages in British quilt history there was a fashion for heavy embroidery on patchwork to enhance plain fabrics. The fashion faded when printed fabrics became the popular materials for quiltmaking. Amongst the few surviving items of patchwork from the early 18th century are a coverlet and a coverlet fragment, which are extensively embellished together with added embroidered and appliquéd motifs known as slips.[5] The coverlet and the fragment were pieced from a variety of silks and velvets and,

whilst some of the fabrics are fancy decorative weave silks, many are brightly coloured but plain woven. The strong tradition in both professional and domestic embroidery of that time is reflected in these two patchwork pieces.

Later in the 18th century, fashionable printed cottons and linens came to be 'shown-off' in patchwork, so the distraction of added pattern was not desirable. An exception was Broderie Perse coverlets and quilts, where embroidery was often added (see the Tree of Life coverlet on page 106).

Pure patchwork without embroidery continued to be the preferred style into the 19th century. It was only when there was a move back to using silks and velvets later in that century that embellishment again became popular in British patchwork. The luxurious silks, velvets and ribbons used for Crazy, Log Cabin and Mosaic patchwork on showy table covers, throws and coverlets often became a medium for extra decoration. Such ostentatious, heavily embroidered surfaces chimed well with the furnishing style of the richer classes.

The striking complex silk and velvet frame quilt shown here is an example of such decoration. Made by Mrs Mills in 1887 to celebrate Queen Victoria's Golden Jubilee, it was sewn for a family in lieu of rent. The entire quilt is covered in embroidery and the outer border of fans in particular contains flowers, animals and figures including fashionable ladies and children playing with toys.

In the second half of the 19th century, quilters could find embroidery stitches and designs in ladies' magazines and needlework books.[6] The stitches were worked in a variety of threads and, in Crazy patchwork, were often accompanied by buttons, braids, beads and sequins to add extra sparkle.

Silk and velvet Jubilee Quilt, *202 x 204cm (79 x 80in),* made by Mrs Mills in 1887 to celebrate Queen Victoria's Golden Jubilee

MAKING FRACTURE

Linda normally makes quilts using cotton and linen, but here she used a wider range of hand-dyed and painted fabrics. The construction of Fracture was straightforward; fabric pieces were placed randomly but with thought given to colour and tone, and sewn down on to a backing. Linda layered much of the quilt with fine gauge net in colours to match the colour changes across the quilt. Some of the net was then cut back to provide extra texture. She used the grass motif across the quilt, stitching it both by hand and machine in mostly self-coloured threads but making it more obvious nearer to the fracture line by using contrasting colours. To give stability and prevent the quilt sagging along the fracture, the top was layered and machine sewn on to a backing.

Linda used three disparate design sources to create her quilt: 'I saw parallels with the fragmented shapes present in all three, the final piece is the coming together of these apparently diverse strands. It was intended as a one-off for this project, but I am inspired to make more work in a similar vein.'

Fracture by Linda Kemshall, 98 x 146cm (38½ x 57½in)

Wholecloth Quilt, *170 x 258cm (67 x 102in)*, with central oval medallion c. 1920s

The simple cream cotton sateen fabric of this wholecloth quilt (opposite) has been transformed into a striking bedcover by the complex design of its hand quilting. Made in a style often described as central medallion and border, it is typical of quilts made in the north east of England in the late 19th and early 20th centuries and was probably made in the 1920s. It carries a small handwritten label 'Mrs Maughan £3.5.0 [£3.25]', which may indicate that it was made to order.

The centre of the quilt contains a defined oval enclosing a complex combination of quilt motifs. The outer border of repeating curved leaf motifs is also illustrated in a paper on the quilt designers of north east England.[1] The quilt has never been used and bears only the marks of being folded for years and blue pencil marking the design.

WHOLECLOTH QUILT
SHEENA NORQUAY

The Wholecloth Quilt (opposite) provided Sheena Norquay with the challenge of designing a sampler of grids suitable for free machine quilting. In designing her three-panel quilt, CGP Panels, she explored the possibilities of traditional infill patterns and chose threads in beiges, greens and blues as a link back to the blue pencil marks on north-country quilts.

'Whenever an idea comes into my head, I scribble ideas and do quick sketches. I love doodling with lines.'

SHEENA NORQUAY

Over the last 20 years, Sheena has made the journey from primary school teacher to freelance quilt teacher and lecturer, with a reputation for striking quilts exhibited widely in national exhibitions. She learned to sew as a child: 'I was drawn to quilting for its sculptural quality and the way it can add movement and texture as well as shapes and motifs to cloth.'

Sheena's two preferred quiltmaking techniques have influenced the style of her quilts. She has produced a series of complex appliqué designs often connected to mythology and her home in the Orkney Islands. Going Home (below right), made for The Quilters' Guild's Nineties Collection, refers to Sheena having to cross the sea to the Islands. 'I sit on the beach as a mermaid with my two cats gazing longingly at the distant land, surrounded by symbols referring to the sea, legends, hope, patience and the passage of time until I can return.' Complex free machine quilting is her other love. She uses it to both enhance appliqué designs and to make striking wholecloth quilts, often laid out sampler style and coupled with subtle changes of colour through softly coloured machine quilting thread, printing and stencilling.

SCRIBBLING, DOODLING AND DRAWING

Sheena's notebook lives with her at all times – beside her bed and when travelling. 'Whenever an idea comes into my head, I scribble ideas and do quick sketches. I love doodling with lines.' For a pictorial piece, 'I usually do research and mull it over for a while before making it. With an experimental piece, I think about options for techniques, fabrics and layout. Again I make lists of ideas to choose from.'

She has been experimenting with grids for some time, including a combination of printed dots, rings and decorative lines within the restriction of a grid or block. She sketches and then accurately draws the patterns, which she will reproduce in her wholecloth quilts, as samplers of simple repeated shapes (see page 79).

Details of the Wholecloth Quilt showing *far right* the border pattern and Square Diamond infill and *near right* the centre detail

Quilt Stampers of the North East of England

From the second half of the 19th century into the mid-20th century, a localized industry of quilt designing flourished in the north east of England. Individuals earned a living by marking quilt designs on quilt tops, generally for wholecloth quilts, but also for strippy and pieced quilts. Blue pencil was used to mark the quilting lines and the similarity of this effect to blue stamped transfer patterns for embroidery might have led to the description, used colloquially, of quilt 'stampers'.[2]

The designers received wholecloth and pieced tops (see Triple X Quilt on page 21) from quilters across the north east or provided their own marked tops for sale. The standard cost for marking was still only 1/6d (7½p) until the 1930s.[3] The designed quilts are distinguished by a complex combination of motifs in the centre of the quilt, a wide flowing border that is broken at the corners by different groups of motifs and Square Diamond infill across the remaining body of the quilt. They stand out against other wholecloth quilts from the area, which also may have been marked in blue, because of the quality of the design and the skilled and confident way the designs, and particularly the infill, were drawn. The designers worked with their own favourite quilt motifs on templates, which they supplemented with extensive freehand drawing of flowers, leaves, stems and scrolls. The quilting motifs had a distinctive regional style and were often based on nature, with formalized flower and leaf designs together with feathers, shells and chain patterns. Two unique designs have been noted. An oval shape described as a flat iron is usually infilled with a rose, leaf and scroll pattern. The other is a freehand drawn open scroll with an added plumed outline, a variation of which can be seen in the Wholecloth Quilt with central oval medallion (see pages 74 and 76).[4]

The designers were based in two valleys, Weardale and Allendale, in the north Pennine dales of Northumberland and County Durham. The establishment of the quilt designing trade is ascribed to a George Gardiner, a draper in Allenheads, Allendale, who trained local girls to quilt and mark quilts probably from the 1870–80s.[5] One of his apprentices, Elizabeth Sanderson, carried on designing and marking quilts in Allenheads until her death in 1933. She took in her own live-in apprentices from the last decade of the 19th century and although few quilts can be attributed to her hand, her influence over the development of the quilt style cannot be denied. However, a Star frame-pieced design can be attributed to her.[6] Generally white with another colour such as red, blue or pink, this striking design was widely available from quilt designers or bought from travelling salesmen.

Another professional quilt marker was Miss Mary Fairless, who continued to mark quilts until retiring in her 80s in 1989.[7] At the age of 19 she had worked with a Mrs Peart, who had been apprenticed to Elizabeth Sanderson, learning to be a pattern marker, and had then continued alone, maintaining a tradition that has flourished since the last quarter of the 19th century.

GRIDS AND SQUARE DIAMONDS

The infill between the quilt patterns in old wholecloth quilts tends to be overlooked. However, the ubiquitous Square Diamond infill (also called Hanging Diamond) seen in north-country wholecloths is very difficult to draw accurately. Well drawn, it is one of the features that distinguishes quilts marked by a quilt stamper. The style of these quilts allows for large areas of infill, which enhance the complex groupings of patterns around them.

During other periods of British quilting and in other regions, the infill has been treated in different ways. In the Cockburn wholecloth quilt (see page 78), made earlier in the 19th century, lines separate the complex central circle design from the borders, and the infill does not link the different areas together. Other infill patterns such as Clamshell were used and can be seen on the wholecloth quilt from Hawick made by Mrs Janet Pow in the 1920–30s (see page 23).

Going Home by Sheena Norquay, 62 x 63cm (24½ x 25in), commissioned for The Quilters' Guild Nineties Collection

Cockburn wholecloth quilt, 228 x 240cm (90 x 94½in), from the second quarter of the 19th century

Sheena was drawn to the infill in old quilts, 'I wanted to set myself a challenge to design and make a sampler of grids suitable for free machine quilting. I looked at the features of infill patterns in old quilts and listed straight lines (crossing diagonals or horizontal and vertical), curved lines in Clamshell and Wineglass, equal spacing of lines, diagonals crossing at different angles to make squares or diamonds, fabrics often with a sheen and threads matching or slightly darker.' From

the list, Sheena chose a curved line, wanting to see how many pattern variations she could draw whilst still making it easy to sew on the machine.

'I set myself some parameters so my drawings could keep a feel for the features of traditional infill pattern using regular spacing to the grids in three different scales. I wanted to concentrate on variety in pattern design using curved lines.' Sheena drew designs in three different sized blocks – 7.6cm

(3in), 15.2cm (6in) and 30.4cm (12in) – allowing one size of spacing in the smallest block, two in the middle-sized block and three in the largest block. She created diagonal grid patterns for the largest block, horizontal and vertical patterns in the middle-sized block and a mix of both for the smallest block.

She said: 'This was quite absorbing when playing with the pattern possibilities, but a bit monotonous to draw out the small-scale grids on the 30.4cm (12in) block. I decided at that stage to break up some of these patterns on the 30.4cm (12in) block to add a bit of interest by adding, subtracting and changing some of the lines. I also planned to flatten some areas within the grid with heavy stitching when I got to the machining stage. The designing and drawing of the grid took 19 hours.'

25 by Sheena Norquay, *100 x 100cm (39½ x 39½in)*

STITCHED SAMPLES

Sheena chose fabrics that had a subtle sheen – cotton sateen, silk cotton mix, silk and satin. She discarded the silk cotton mix after it shrank when she wet and ironed it. She stitched samples of the grids using the remaining three fabrics, experimenting with different machine needles and threads. 'Satin distorts when machined in larger pieces so I decided to use it for the smallest blocks only. I would use silk dupion for the 15.2cm (6in) block and sateen for the largest blocks.'

The original plan was to make a frame-style sampler with a square of 7.6cm (3in) blocks in the centre surrounded by borders of the other two sizes of block. 'Because of the distortion problem, I decided to change to three panels made up of the three sizes of blocks.'

MACHINE QUILTING

Free machine quilting is done by dropping the feed dogs in the sewing machine, setting the stitch length to '0' and using a darning or quilting foot. 'I do all my quilting using a 25.5cm

Drawings of the grids

Stitched samples: experiments with fabric and thread

MARKING AND MACHINING

Successful quilting can only be achieved after careful marking of the design on the fabric. Sheena did not want the marks to be obvious, so she traced the design using a propelling pencil, resorting to a light box for the more intricate patterns. She chose a number of pale pastel shades for the threads, including beiges, greens and blues; the subtle colouring of the stitching was a link back to the blue pencil marks of north-country quilts. 'On some of the larger grids, I flattened different areas of the background with heavy stitching to add interest to the block and show the various ways it could be quilted. I quilted the grids from top to bottom on each panel, working the grid lines in straight and satin stitch and then separating the blocks with satin stitch.

Quilting the grids took about 13 hours. The extra quilting, trimming thread ends and binding the panels took me another 24 hours.'

NAMING THE PANELS

'Before I finished quilting the panels, I had to have my last remaining cat put down, so many tears were shed during the final quilting and completion of the panels. It occurred to me at this time to call the panels the CGP Panels in memory of my cats, who have brought me so much pleasure over the last 11 years. I have quilted a cat together with its name on each panel – Cuddles, Garfield and Persistence. This was the last piece of work 'supervised' by Cuddles. You may still find one of her hairs somewhere on the panels.'

(10in) hoop, but you can use just your hands to hold the quilt layers.' Attaching the three layers of the quilt 'sandwich' together firmly is important. 'I tacked (basted) the panels in vertical and horizontal lines approximately 5cm (2in) apart.' Other quilters prefer to pin the layers together.

It is important to try samples of fabric, wadding (batting), thread and needles before starting so that materials can be rejected if unsuitable, as Sheena discovered with the silk and cotton mix fabric. Wadding (batting) can be a significant influence over the final result and a firm, but thinner thickness is best. For this project, Sheena chose Hobbs wool wadding (batting). She was prepared to cope with frequent changes of needles and thread in order to achieve the best effect. 'I used Madeira cotton tanne no. 50 with a machine quilting needle, Mettler no. 100 with a size 10 jeans needle and Sulky metallic thread with a metallica or heavy metal needle.

Detail of CGP Panels, showing machine-quilted grids and Sheena's cat

CGP Panels by Sheena Norquay, *30.5 x 137cm (12 x 54in), 30.5 x 152.5cm (12 x 60in), 30.5 x 137cm (12 x 54in)*

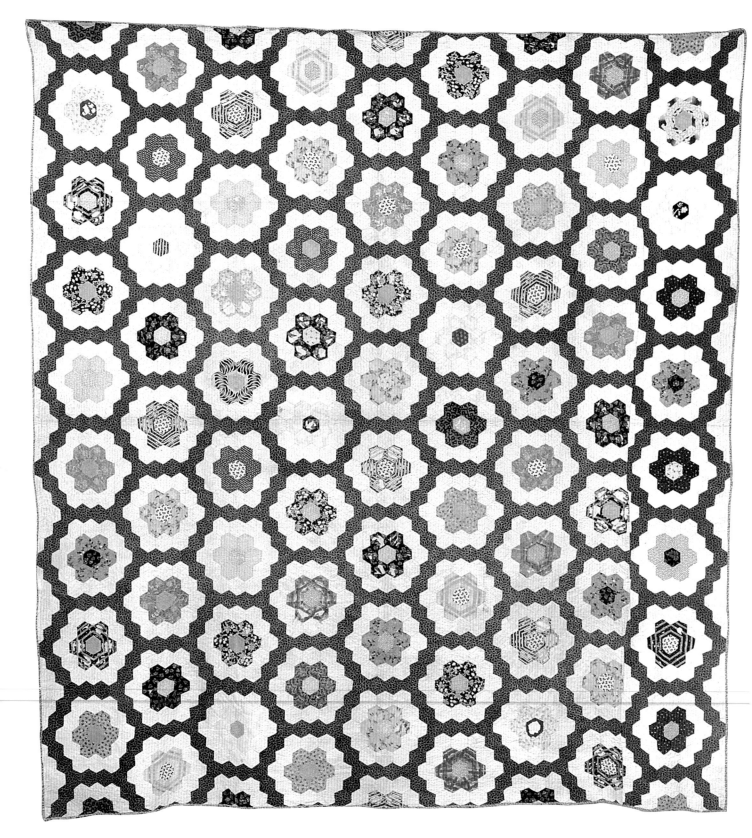

Manchester Hexagon Quilt, *224 x 239cm (88 x 94in)*, mid-19th century

The hexagon quilt (opposite), made in the mid-19th century, was found in the Manchester area in northern England. Owned by Helen Stewart Watt of Arbroath, Scotland, who was born in around 1863–64, it is made from printed and plain cottons with double rosettes of hexagons linked by a surrounding row or 'path' of pink and blue hexagons in a pattern sometimes called Grandmother's Flower Garden. At some stage, the quilt was damaged on the right side and it has been rejoined with the loss of part of the second vertical row of rosettes.

Because the hexagon shape tessellates with other hexagons to form a mosaic pattern, it offers various design opportunities. A simple pattern of single rosettes is made from six hexagons placed around a central hexagon. This can be developed into more complex designs such as that shown on the coverlet from c. 1870s (see page 84).

HEXAGON QUILT
DAVINA THOMAS

Intrigued by the hexagon shape and the contrast of paper templates framed by fabric turnings, Davina Thomas used computer software to design her contemporary hexagon quilt, Fragments of Time 1 (right). Scanned images were distorted by warping and twirling; various scales of hexagon shapes and patterns, washed with soft colours, were computer-printed directly on to fabric for the hexagon centres.

DAVINA THOMAS

Davina has two very different skills that she can apply to her quiltmaking; she grew up knowing how to sew and, having worked extensively in IT, can use a computer as a design tool. She tried patchwork when she was about 10 years old and took it up again as a late teenager, making her first quilt for her parents aged 21. Davina took the City and Guilds Embroidery course whilst in full-time employment and then fitted in the Patchwork and Quilting course around maternity leave and in the evenings. After teaching quilting for a time, she is now a contributing editor to a quilting magazine. Davina's preference is for piecing and, if forced to choose one technique, she declares: 'I would be happy to sew half-square triangles for the rest of my life.'

'I would be happy to sew half-square triangles for the rest of my life.'

COMPUTER WORK

Davina claims to have no drawing skills. 'I cannot even draw a square by hand and have to use a computer to line things up. "Doodling" in sketchbooks is not for me because I tend to lose my sketches – my impatient nature is more suited to computer design work where I can change colour or shape very easily at the click of a mouse.'

Since Davina is happiest when sitting at her computer, her research and design work is done this way. She analyses a theme by first looking up words in a dictionary, consulting a thesaurus for variations and researching further information on the Internet. Davina then moves on to a variety of software design programmes using Quilt-Pro for simple block or frame designs, Serif PhotoPlus (other photo-editing programmes can be used) for distorting images, and Serif DrawPlus and PagePlus for yet further drawing and colouring.

The hexagon shape intrigues Davina. She realized that, with a shape of six equal sides, there was

Coverlet, *253 x 278cm (97 x 109in)*, c.1870, printed cotton